Guinea Pigs

Guinea Pigs

AN OWNER'S GUIDE TO CHOOSING, RAISING, BREEDING, AND SHOWING

by HARRIETT RUBINS
illustrated by PAMELA CARROLL

Lothrop, Lee & Shepard Books
New York

Text copyright © 1982 by Harriett Rubins
Illustrations copyright © 1982 by Pam Carroll
All rights reserved. No part of this book may be reproduced or utilized in any form or by any means, electronic or mechanical, including photocopying, recording or by any information storage and retrieval system, without permission in writing from the Publisher. Inquiries should be addressed to Lothrop, Lee & Shepard Books, a division of William Morrow & Company, Inc., 105 Madison Avenue, New York, New York 10016. Printed in the United States of America. First Edition.

1 2 3 4 5 6 7 8 9 10

Library of Congress Cataloging in Publication Data

Rubins, Harriett.
   Guinea pigs, an owner's guide to choosing, raising, breeding, and showing.

   Bibliography: p.
   Includes index.
   Summary: Discusses the characteristics of the guinea pig, or cavy, and gives advice on choosing and caring for a pet, as well as breeding and showing.
   1. Guinea pigs as pets—Juvenile literature. [1. Guinea pigs] I. Carroll, Pamela, ill. II. Title.
SF459.G9R8   636'.93234   82-231
ISBN 0-688-01430-5   AACR2

*To my father,
who would have loved this book,
and to Josh*

CONTENTS

1	CHOOSING YOUR PET	11
2	HOME SWEET HOME	35
3	WHAT TO EAT	43
4	KEEPING OR GETTING YOUR PIG IN THE PINK	51
5	TO BREED OR NOT TO BREED: PROBLEMS AND REWARDS	73
6	PREDICTING THE OFFSPRING: HOW TO GET WHAT	91
7	SHOW TIME!	111
8	WANT MORE INFORMATION?	129
	INDEX	140

ACKNOWLEDGMENTS

I would like to thank some of the many people who have helped me on the long journey through the writing of this book. My friends from the New York State Cavy Fanciers, Fay Dumbleton, John Kramer, Lois McNulty, Flo Caldwell, Sheila Schwartz, Nancy Lichtenstein, Bill Felicita, and the rest, inspired and sustained my interest in the project, always ready and willing to give advice and support. The wonderful members of the Ontario Cavy Club, especially Bruce Eisel, the Jim Meade family, Gwynne Hyland, Rae Wilkins, Monika Hildebrandt, John and Ursula Webbing, the Mansefields, and the others, graciously allowed me to scrutinize and photograph their prize cavies. These people continuously extended their friendship and hospitality to me and to the many 4-H'ers I dragged along to their shows.

A special thanks goes to Murray and Donna Platt of Vancouver, British Columbia, for the numerous beautiful photographs from which studies and drawings were made, for their excellent suggestions, and for sharing information with me about their cavy experiences.

Stuart Gluckman, D.V.M., was an inspiration. He kept me smiling when I bogged down, and he helped fill in the gaps and made sure I kept things clear and simple. John Kramer, Ph.D., and Harry Claus also reviewed the manuscript and offered many constructive criticisms.

Finally, the biggest thanks goes to my husband and family, who all loved this latest project of mine. They read each page and eagerly awaited the final results. Here it is, with love.

> Harriett Rubins
> Haligonian Farm, March 1982

1
CHOOSING YOUR PET

Guinea pigs—or cavies, as they are called by serious fanciers—are all-purpose pets. They are like other pets in many ways. Fido the dog will greet you when you come home with wonderfully sloppy licks and body wiggles. Sasha the cat purrs and rubs her body against your legs saying, "Pick me up, love me and feed me. I'm glad you're back!" Porky the guinea pig will whistle his hello just as joyfully, sometimes standing on his hind legs, sometimes pacing back and forth waiting for a pat or a ride in your arms. Porky will also sit quietly in your lap as you watch television or read a book, just as Fido and Sasha might do. With a small piece of lettuce or carrot you can teach your cavy a whole bunch of tricks, such as sitting up and begging, shaking paws, or lying on his back and playing dead—a feat few guinea pigs will do unless they really trust you. And cavies have added bonuses. They are friendly toward people and respond well to the smallest kindnesses. A gentle rub, a brief cuddle, a snip of carrot will keep Porky happy and lovable. These little pets won't take your toys, shred the homework that you were doing on the floor, or scratch furniture or you. And they don't have to be exercised. But if you happen to have some extra time and love to spend on them, they'll literally squeak for joy.

Some people say that cavies are dumb animals. It is

true, they are not usually animated or nervous pets. You'd have to classify them as sitters rather than doers. They seem to prefer watching the world go by to running, jumping, climbing, or cavorting. But dumb they're not. Our cavy Princess learned to sit up and beg for lettuce. She would put her paw in my daughter's hand when asked, and even whistled shrilly when the children came in the front door after school. Our friend's cavy, Marshy, had other talents—she did the hula, grass skirt and all.

WHEN CAVIES CAME TO OUR HOUSE

Our family began our "herd" of guinea pigs in 1971. One of my daughter's friends asked us if we would babysit for Pudgie Pig, her red-and-white, roly-poly guinea pig. We said we would and that was the start of it all. Pudgie was wonderful. She lived in a twenty-gallon aquarium in the kitchen. When the refrigerator door opened, she would rise up on her hind legs and, resting her chin on the top of the glass, soulfully stare and whistle at the person opening the door. How could I, or anyone else, not give her a piece of carrot or apple? Pudgie loved to be held and was always cavylike and gentle. After she went home, we went out and bought our own guinea pigs: Princess, Toastie, and Sam. They were terrific pets, and friends, too. They, in time, had babies, which we raised and for which we later found homes.

By accident, we met another cavy owner. She was a very serious breeder. From her we found out that there are many different types and colors of guinea pigs and that people show cavies much as cat fanciers do. From our new friend we also found out that it is relatively easy to learn about genetics by raising guinea pigs, because cavies mature and breed at an early age.

Within two years we had gained many more guinea pigs. I was showing, breeding, and selling a great number of them. Their ranks increased until we had to move them from the house to a room in the garage. Later, we moved to a larger home with land enough for a barn. The cavies, their numbers having swelled to almost three hundred, lived in their own heated room in the barn, next to the rabbits, chickens, kittens, and horses that were quickly filling up all the wonderful space we thought we would have when we originally planned the animal house.

I did some color and breed studies, as well as experiments with light and nutrition. We even did a study on sicknesses when a very bad respiratory disease struck our cavy herd. It was great fun having all those pets. It was also a lot of work making sure each animal had the best care possible. In addition they had to have enough love and attention to keep them friendly and happy.

I gained enough experience with the many animals at our Haligonian Farm to work at an animal hospital as a veterinary technician. This and my job as a county 4-H Rabbit and Cavy Club leader allow me to do the things I love the most—work with animals and children.

These days, our cavy herd has only a few dozen members, all of them characters. Boreman the clown grabs our schnauzer, Super Dog, by the beard and tries to pull him into his cage. Fruitcake climbs and hangs on the sides of the cage—one of the few cavies I know of that climbs at all. Harmony, a direct descendant of our original Princess, licks like a puppy. I could go on. They are all different. Many are unforgettable.

If you decide to add cavies to your family, this book should answer all your questions—the questions that beginning cavy owners and breeders always seem to ask me. My family and I really enjoy guinea pigs, and the more you know about them, the more you'll be able to enjoy yours.

IS A GUINEA PIG RIGHT FOR YOU?

I was introduced to some tiny, soft, furry creatures called "Tribbles" during an episode of the television show *Star Trek*. They did nothing but look adorable and, of course, reproduce. And years ago in the "Li'l Abner" comic strip, I read about the lovable, pear-shaped "Shmoos," who adored people and had no purpose in life but to be cute, friendly, and edible.

Well, just like the Tribbles and Shmoos, guinea pigs are soft, furry, cuddly, and cute, often thought of as living teddy bears. But, also like those irresistible creatures, they're practically defenseless. When frightened, they freeze in place more often than they run. So, though cavies seem to enjoy being held, and thrive on any amount of gentle handling, you must be ready and willing to accept the responsibility of caring for them and protecting them from other pets in the house and from other children too young to know how to treat them properly. For example, guinea pigs may wiggle if they are uncomfortable. And when a baby cavy squirms in a small brother's or sister's hand, he or she may either grasp it too tightly or let the little pet fall. Unfortunately, a dropped guinea pig is usually a dead guinea pig. Also keep in mind that, while easily housed and fed, guinea pigs cannot be housebroken. To prevent unwanted little puddles and piles on you or on the

A new pet is a commitment—love returns love.

family rugs, cavies must be returned to their cages periodically to urinate and defecate in their bedding. One final consideration: guinea pigs do shed. Although they shed no more than a dog or a cat, someone who has many allergies may have a bad reaction to cavy hair.

If cost is a factor in your choice of a pet, guinea pigs should be near the top of the list. Humane societies often have a few available for adoption. Friends or friends of friends usually know someone with extra guinea pigs. Pet shops sell young cavies for as little as five dollars, though the rarer animals may go for as much as twenty to fifty dollars. Feeding costs will vary from place to place, depending on the availability of pellets, grains, and vegetables. But, you can probably figure on slightly more than a few cents a day.

With any pet, and especially with cavies, the major

deciding factor should be how great the desire for that pet really is. Cavies are friendly and outgoing. They love company and attention. A lonesome guinea pig sits like a lump in the corner of his cage. So try to be certain that you won't lose interest a short time after the cavy's arrival. Who suggested the pet in the first place? For what reasons? Check your motives and make sure that this cavy is wanted! A pet of any kind requires *total commitment.*

FINDING THEIR ROOTS

Guinea pigs aren't pigs. And they don't come from Guinea. So why are they called "guinea pigs"? The label "pig" may have come about when early Spanish settlers saw great numbers of short-coated cavies in the marketplaces of South America and compared them to suckling pigs, since both animals were prepared for eating in the same way (by scalding and scraping). Also, the sound made by guinea pigs when they're frightened is similar to a pig's squeal. The name "guinea" possibly arose from the price, one guinea, of the little creatures brought to England by sailors. However, a more likely explanation is that Europeans were more used to ships arriving from New Guinea than from other countries and mistakenly tagged the animals "guinea pigs."

What about the term "cavy"? One theory is that it is derived from the animal's official scientific name, Cavia porcellus. In Latin, *Cavia* signifies the special group of animals to which guinea pigs belong while *porcellus* translates as "little pig." It is more likely, however, that the term stems from the guinea pig's original South American Indian name, "cabiai."

To help them in their studies, scientists have developed a system of grouping, or classifying, all living things according to what they have in common. The two biggest classification groups are plants and animals. These two huge groups are then divided into smaller groups, such as fish, reptiles, amphibians, birds, and mammals. These are further divided into still more specialized groups.

People are mammals; so are guinea pigs. But guinea pigs are in a different mammalian subgroup, or family, from humans: people are in the primate family; cavies are members of the rodent family. Rodents have in common front teeth, used for gnawing, that grow throughout their lives. Cavies are more closely related to such rodents as the American woodchuck, the South American chinchilla, and the porcupine than they are

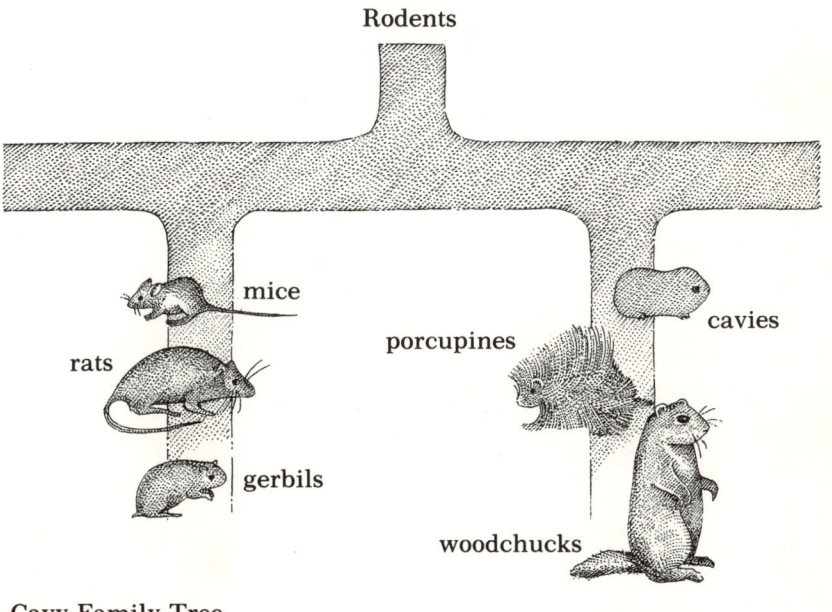

Cavy Family Tree

to rats, mice, and gerbils, rodents to which guinea pigs are most often compared. In fact, guinea pigs belong to a different family subgroup from rats, mice, and gerbils because their appearances, dispositions, and habits are so dissimilar.

TAKING A CLOSER LOOK, OR WHO'S WHO IN THE CAVY WORLD

In most cases, guinea pigs are compact little animals, weighing between two and three pounds at maturity. They are tailless, so if someone tells you that picking up a cavy by the tail will cause his eyes to fall out, don't believe it. You're having your leg pulled. All cavies have three toes on their rear feet and four on their front, though, occasionally, a youngster turns up with a tiny fourth toe on its hind feet.

Cavies use many different sounds to express their feelings. Among these are a shrill calling whistle, a purring mating song, a frightened squeal, and a soft, contented chirping.

There are differences, however, in guinea pig size and shape, hair color and style, and personality, depending upon the animal's breed, sex, and variety (or coloring). Only six breeds, or types, of cavies are now recognized by the American Rabbit Breeders Association (ARBA) and the American Cavy Breeders Association (ACBA), the national voices of cavy fanciers across the United States. These are the American, Abyssinian, Peruvian, White Crested, Teddy, and Silkie. The newer breeds (today's Teddies, White Cresteds, and Silkies) were developed from mutations, or variations (see chapter 6), of the three earlier breeds. Although examples of the newer types were reported as long ago as the 1930s, serious breeding has been a very recent development. The Silkie, for example, was officially shown for the first time only in 1979.

To help you decide which guinea pig is right for you, let's first take a look at each breed and then some of the common cavy varieties.

The **American** cavy is the original breed, the one developed from the wild guinea pigs that were domesticated and raised as food in South America hundreds of years ago. Their coloring, coat features, and shape have changed little over the years. Then they were usually agouti-colored, having deep-red hair with black tips. Their coats were, and still are, soft and short (not more than three-quarters to one inch long) and very smooth. Resembling tiny blimps or footballs, Americans are what most people think of when guinea pigs are mentioned. The white variety of American is the guinea pig most used in laboratories, mainly because there are no frills and the fewest variables—just a smooth, compact body.

Ideal American

If you are interested in a pure-bred American cavy, look for an elliptical body, slightly round at the rear and just slightly longer in the face, that is of medium length—about ten to twelve inches. The animal should have large bold eyes, a rounded nose (not a pointed, or needle, nose), and drooping, but not drooped or crinkled, ears. At full growth, Americans weigh two and a half to three pounds, though lately some breeders have been developing much heavier animals, some tipping the scales at over four pounds.

The **Abyssinian** cavy is thought to have first appeared in England. As early as the mid-1800s, scientists and fanciers were describing the breed and trying to determine its origin. The distinguishing feature of the "Abby," as it is commonly called, is its medium-short, wiry coat that grows in a remarkable rosette, or swirl, pattern. Sometimes it takes a trained eye to realize that, in a healthy, perfect Abby, there is real organization to all those swirls. If you look closely, you should be able to count ten evenly spaced rosettes, which are separated by a mane between the ears to the base of the neck,

Ideal Abby

a collar from shoulder to shoulder, and two ridges. Abbys seem to be a little more animated and slightly less sedentary than the Americans. Surprisingly, even though they have coat hair about one inch long, they require no more grooming than the short-haired Americans and White Cresteds.

What should you look for in an Abyssinian? An adult Abby should weigh over two pounds and have a slightly smaller and narrower body than the American breed. Its head should have a more prominent nose than either an American or a White Crested, as well as a definite mustache. The ten rosettes should be placed this way: four in line across the saddle, or middle, of the animal, four at the base of the back on the rump and hips, and one on each shoulder. The mane, collar, and two ridges should stand erect. An Abby's medium-short coat is extremely coarse and feels bristly when stroked.

The **Peruvian** cavy is the longest-coated breed, with hair that grows about one inch or more during every month of its life. It is often considered to be the elite of the guinea pig world because of the great care and pampering needed to preserve and protect this luxurious coat. Peruvians are thought to have been first seen in France. Scientists writing about this breed in the 1800s described it as having originated earlier in Peru or Brazil and being developed in France as a fancy. It is easy to imagine these unusual moppets belonging in the elegance of Parisian society.

Today's Peruvian enthusiast or showperson keeps the eighteen- to twenty-inch-long coats tied up in endpapers called wrappers, which are removed as often as once a day for comb-outs. At a cavy show, the Peruvian sits on a specially designed platform that presents the dense, soft, sweeping, and silky coat in such a way that

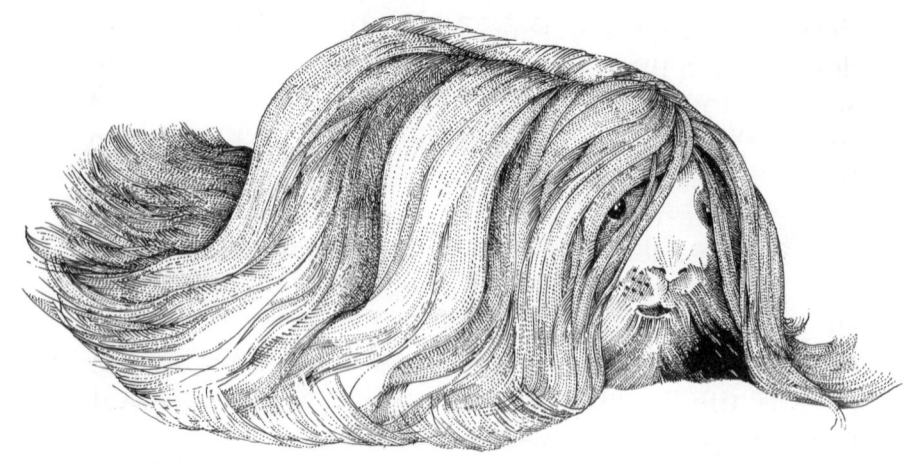

Ideal Peruvian

it's sometimes difficult to know which end of the guinea pig is which. And, so they won't spoil this effect, show Peruvians are trained to stand perfectly still for long periods of time.

But this much grooming and care are not really necessary for the pet owner. As long as wrappers are not used, the Peruvian's coat will stay relatively short (four or five inches) because of knotting, matting, the cavy's chewing on his own coat, or his coat's being chewed on by a roommate. Brushing or combing two or three times a week should keep the pet's coat perfectly soft and unsnarled. If cost is a factor in your selection, you should know that Peruvians are usually more expensive than other breeds, perhaps because they often have smaller litters and are thus less readily available. This does not seem to have stopped many teenage girls, however, for whom Peruvians are an especially popular breed.

The most important feature of the pure-bred

Peruvian is its coat. It should be soft in texture and very dense. When properly combed, the coat is divided into sections: those hairs growing over the rump are called the rear sweeps; those growing from the sides of the body are the side sweeps; and the hairs combed forward and growing from the top of the head are called the frontal. These sections should be even in length all the way around so that, when viewed from above, there should be no hint of which end of the animal is front or back. With an adult weight of between two and three pounds, the Peruvian should have a body rounded at both ends, and, like the American, have big bold eyes and drooping ears.

The **White Cresteds** are a more recently recognized breed. First developed in Canada and then the United States, they were officially accepted by the national cavy and rabbit breeders' organizations in 1973 after their annual convention in Detroit, but were not allowed to be shown until the *Standards of Perfection* was published in 1974. White Cresteds resemble their American ancestors with their short, silky coats, large limpid eyes, rounded noses, and sturdily compact bodies. The difference, however, lies in the crest, for which they are named: a beautiful white rosette that is centered between and in front of their ears. Although White Cresteds can be bred for many different colors, a solid red coat with a white crest is the most common variety.

The perfect White Crested has the same body shape and coat as the American breed. The crest should contain the only white hairs on the animal's body. It should be in the middle of the forehead behind the eyes and in front of the ears, with the hairs radiating evenly all around the center point.

The **Teddy** is the newest breed, having been officially recognized for showing by the American Cavy Breeders Association in 1978. Teddies were developed as a mutation from Americans and are similar to them in every feature except for their coats. Baby Teddies look as if they have Afro hairstyles with bushy coats and frizzled whiskers.

The ideal Teddy has a body and head like the ideal American's and a coat that is extremely coarse, harsh, and dense. Teddy fur is short and thick, and usually grows only about one-half inch in length. Teddies' kinky coats and curled whiskers make them quite an appealing breed.

The **Silkie**—or Sheltie, as it is called in England, where it has been an accepted breed for many years—has been recognized in the United States for showing only since 1979. Therefore, it is debatable whether the Silkie should be considered a new or an old breed. In any case, it is a regal breed. It also has the body shape and facial features of the American cavy, but its coat, like the Peruvian's, continues to grow throughout its life. Unlike the Peruvian coat, however, the Silkie's is combed toward the rear of the animal (rather than forward) as it grows. This means that the groomed Silkie has no frontal so that the overhead view reminds you of a teardrop. Even when they're at rest, the long-haired Silkies appear to be flowing or sweeping forward, as if the wind were whipping at their tresses.

When shopping for a perfect Silkie, look for a body like any good-quality American cavy's and a coat that is long, soft, and silky with side and rear sweeps that are as dense and even as a Peruvian's. There must be no trace of the frontal hairs covering the nose and eyes from view: all hairs must grow and be combed toward the animal's rear.

Ideal White Crested

Ideal Teddy

Ideal Silkie

BREED CHARACTERISTICS

Breed	Body shape	Facial features
AMERICAN	elliptical	large, bold eyes; rounded nose; drooping ears
ABYSSINIAN	smaller and narrower than American	more prominent nose than American and White Crested; definite mustache
PERUVIAN	rounded at both ends	large, bold eyes; drooping ears
WHITE CRESTED	elliptical	large, limpid eyes; rounded nose
TEDDY	elliptical	large, bold eyes; rounded nose
SILKIE	elliptical	large, bold eyes; rounded nose; drooping ears

Coat	Adult weight
soft, short, very smooth	two and a half to three pounds, though may be four or more
ten rosettes: four across saddle, four at base of back and rump, and one at each shoulder; mane, collar, and ridges erect; medium-short coarse hair, bristly to touch	over two pounds
soft, dense, even all around	two to three pounds
short, silky, with white rosette between the eyes	over two pounds
coarse, harsh coat, hair one-half inch long	two and a half to three pounds
long, soft, silky; dense and even side and rear sweeps; no frontal	two and a half to three pounds

Other breeds are being worked on at this time, including the **Satin**, the **Ridgeback**, and the **Coronation** to name just a few. The Satin's outstanding feature is its coat, which has a unique sheen. Otherwise, it looks very similar to the American and White Crested breeds. The Ridgeback is named for the ridge of hair that runs down the length of its back from the neck to the hind end, the highlight on an otherwise completely smooth coat. Its other characteristics should be the same as for the American breed. The Coronation is basically a Crested Silkie.

VARIETIES

Thanks to nature and the work of cavy breeders, guinea pigs now appear in a gorgeous array of colors, ranging from a single, all-over coloring to a special mixture. New varieties are being developed all the time. Not all breeds are commonly found in all varieties currently recognized by the American Cavy Breeders Association. Blue roan Teddies are rarely seen, for example, and bi-color White Cresteds (two-color, other than white, White Cresteds) are also quite unusual. Before color types are described, remember that labeling is very difficult since people imagine different shades for the same word. For example, a red cavy can be thought of as brown by some people, orange by others, and rust by still others.

Selfs are animals that have only a single body color. The officially recognized colors are beige, black, blue, chocolate, cream, lilac, red, red-eyed orange, and white.

Solids have a mixture of colors, either on the same hair or on adjacent hairs, that give a single-color appearance. A change in color distribution may make a solid-coated cavy look textured or highlighted. Brindles (red mixed with black) and roans (red or black evenly mixed with white) are the most common solids. Other colors recognized by the ACBA include golden, silver, and dilute, all of which are color combinations on the same hair. Golden consists of a red base with black ends; silver is achieved by a white base with black ends; and dilute can be any mixture of cream, orange, red, or white tips on a base of beige, black, chocolate, or lilac.

Agouti is a mixture of two colors on the same hair. The difference between the agouti and the solid is that the agouti's belly hair is only a single color, which matches the base color of the other body hairs. For example, the golden agouti has a red-colored belly, while the silver agouti's belly is white. Golden, silver, and dilute are the colors accepted by the ACBA.

Marked cavies are far and away the brightest and liveliest varieties. These have two or more colors, which appear in definite patches. The Dutch, for example, resembles a little Dutch bunny with white feet, collar, and blaze and a contrasting body color of black or red. The Himalayan has a white body color with black smut on the nose, feet, socks, and ears. Its eyes are always pink. A perfect tortoiseshell has a checkerboard pattern of red and black. The tortoiseshell and white has white patches added to this checkerboard pattern and is to me the most colorful of all. One other marked variety is the Dalmatian, whose white body is dotted with random spots of color.

Broken colors are also very bright and cheery. These cavies can be any combination of two or more colors that aren't solid or agouti mixtures, such as cream and white, or agouti, red, and white.

Black accents highlight the Himalayan's white coat. Its length—too long for an American and to short for a Silkie—would keep him from being a show winner.

The coat pattern of the tortoiseshell and white resembles a checkerboard.

WHICH SEX? WHAT AGE? HOW MANY?

Common question: Which cavies are better as pets, males or females? Answer: They're both fine. Both males (boars) and females (sows) respond well to human contact. You can tell the sex of a cavy by gently turning it belly up. There are two openings. The one nearer the back is the anus. Through this the cavy eliminates feces. The other opening on the male is similar to an X shape. If you press gently on the abdomen

Gently pressing on the cavy's abdomen will tell you if the animal is a boar.

very close to this opening, the boar's penis will protrude. The female's other opening is flatter and more like a Y shape.

No matter the sex, the more attention cavies get, the better they like it. But if a cavy of either sex is raised singly, without cavy companionship, it will usually become possessive of its cage and not take kindly to new cagemates of any sex. So, if you are at school all day, it might be wise to buy a duo of the same sex and, preferably, of approximately the same age. Later on, however, when adding companions, differences in age may be a help: while Big Bruno might not care for Old Sidney to join him in his home, he should readily accept a weanling. Older boars usually welcome the little fellows. An older sow, though, is not quite as adaptable. She likes her privacy and strongly objects to cavy intruders, if she has never had visitors before. Of course, if you decide to breed cavies, you'll need at least one guinea pig of each sex. These should be kept separated until they are old enough and large enough to breed.

But the really exciting part of choosing your cavy is selecting the breed, color, and hairstyle. Do you like the sleek American look, the tousled and swirled Abyssinian, the elegant Peruvian, the comical White Crested? Or maybe even the frizzled Teddy or the rare, graceful Silkie? Perhaps you will want to take your chances and opt for the crossbred animal. In this case, you can guess at the kind of coat the cavy will have when he matures. Decide what look you like best. Then, to avoid being disappointed, check with local breeders and pet shops to find out what breeds and varieties are available in your area.

Male or female, single or pair, your new cavy should be, above all, a healthy animal. When picking out your future pet, look for an active cavy with clear eyes, an alert expression, a smooth, shiny coat, and a sturdy, rounded body.

Of course, whatever you settle on in advance, you may get to the caviary or pet shop and find all your careful decisions totally disregarded in favor of the adorable little baby cavy that jumps into your hand, snuggles down, and seems to be begging you to take him home. Don't feel locked into your initial decision. Take a long look at that friendly, gentle, personable fellow even if he's a little out of the ordinary, a little different from what you originally had in mind. Remember, personality counts, too.

2
HOME SWEET HOME

After you choose your pet, rule number one is to make sure that he or she has a place to come home to so that settling in is as smooth as possible. Guinea pigs are adaptable creatures, being equally happy in a cardboard carton, a fish tank, a crate, or a cage—any place you can keep them dry and clean. Unlike other rodents, they chew very little on wooden or cardboard homes. Just be sure to allow about two square feet of space for a single cavy and at least one additional square foot for each companion.

WOOD OR METAL?

Both wooden and metal cages have advantages and drawbacks. Metal cages can be purchased from pet shops or other pet-product distribution centers. They usually have wire sides and a wire door with either wire or solid floors. Often they have a removable tray on the bottom to make cleaning easier. Metal can be cleaned more thoroughly than wood, and dries quickly. But wood cages are warmer—an important difference if the cage is to be kept in a cool basement or garage. In a house, however, where temperatures do not vary that much, either wood or metal will make a comfortable home for your cavy.

Metal cages are expensive compared to wooden

crates, which are readily and cheaply available from fish stores and supermarkets. A fish crate is large enough to house an adult pair of cavies or a sow and litter, but you will have to put up with the fish odor—temporarily. After a few days of airing or a thorough scraping and sanding, no one will ever know what was originally packed in it.

To prepare a wooden box or crate as a cavy cage, first sand it with coarse sandpaper to remove the rough spots and splinters. Next, use a finer grade of sandpaper to make the floor smooth. With a wide paintbrush (two to three inches), apply one or two coats of spar varnish, easily obtained from any hardware store (the smallest size can will be more than enough for one cage). If the wood is not varnished, it will become saturated with moisture from urine and drips from water bottles or crocks, and will have to be aired, cleaned, and dried periodically. After varnishing, you can cover and decorate the crate with any paint that happens to be around the house, *as long as it is lead-free* (lead is poisonous) *and not water based.*

A door for your cage can be made by cutting four pieces of fir stripping (inexpensive, thin, narrow strips of wood sold at hardware and lumber stores) to the size of one side of the box. Nail these pieces together with tiny brads (nails) to make a frame. Cover the frame with one-inch chicken wire, attaching it with staples. A drop of paper glue or a bit of clay on the sharp ends of the wire will protect both you and your cavy from scratches and jabs. By fastening two hinges to the bottom of the door and the cage, you can make the door drop downward. Or you can connect the top of the door and cage with hinges so the door lifts upward. No one way is better. It's just a matter of what you prefer.

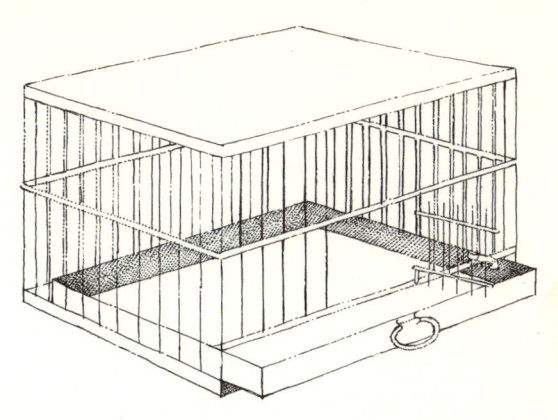

High tray sides in the metal cage prevent shavings from falling out.

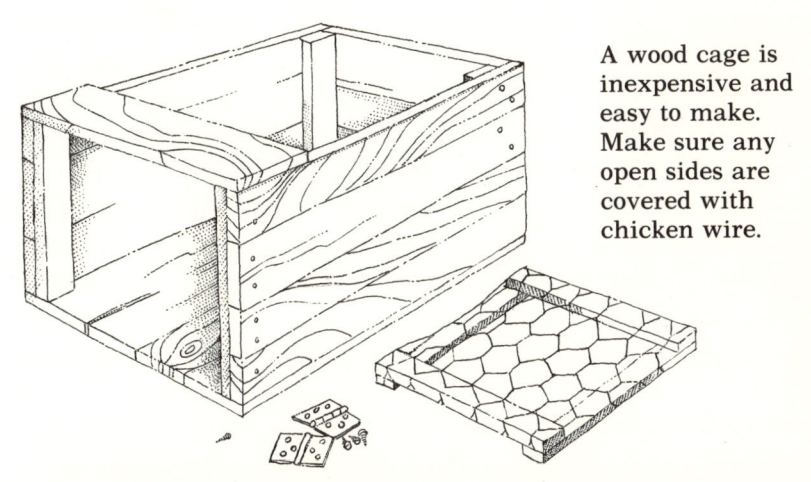

A wood cage is inexpensive and easy to make. Make sure any open sides are covered with chicken wire.

To make sure that your cavy won't push open the door and fall out, you'll need either a latch or a hook-and-eye to keep the door fastened. They are made to be screwed into wood and are sold at all hardware stores.

OR GLASS?

Another very good type of cage is an aquarium. "Leakers," fish tanks that no longer hold water because of leaks or cracks in the glass, can be bought from pet shops or at garage sales for very little money. You won't have to worry about shavings, droppings, or spilled food since these are always contained within the tank. A twenty-gallon aquarium gives a cavy plenty of room in which to run and lots of light. Remember, however, that leaving a pet in an aquarium in daytime heat can be dangerous, particularly in the summertime, since air circulation is poor. Direct sunlight can literally cook him as the rays are intensified through the glass. Care should be taken to provide guinea pigs in any type of cage with shade from the sun.

DECOR OF THE FLOOR

Cages can be made with solid wood or metal floors, removable pans, or wire mesh. So which type is best? Laboratories usually use wire because it is more sanitary and easier to clean. This wire flooring—generally one-half-inch-square hardware cloth—covers a tray, which can be regularly removed, emptied of droppings, and scrubbed.

For pet cavies at home, however, I greatly prefer solid floors. Cavies have been known to break toes or legs while running on wire. They can also get calluses and sore, red feet. A solid floor or a wire floor can be covered with bedding to make it softer, warmer, and easier on cavy feet and legs. Shredded newspapers or pine shavings make fine bedding, with a thick layer of newspapers, edges turned upward, laid down underneath. (Don't worry if your cavy eats a little of the bedding: this is his way of keeping his teeth trimmed.)

Also acceptable, though more expensive, is commercially produced small-pet bedding, which consists of large granules of a claylike substance. Straw is fine, too, but it is not as absorbent as newspaper or pine shavings. Other beddings, though, especially cedar shavings and kitty litter, have been known to cause allergic reactions in some—not all—guinea pigs. (The symptom in such cases is gradual hair loss, most noticeable on the stomach.) Very fine shavings or sawdust are also not advisable since, if eaten, they may cause a digestive block. Furthermore, they can become caked on the toenails and cause irritations.

INSIDE OR OUTSIDE?

Plan to house your cavy indoors for most of the year. Guinea pigs prefer, and do their best, in temperatures ranging from 60 to 80 degrees Fahrenheit. In lower temperatures, they'll need added warmth from straw, hay, or other little cavy bodies they can snuggle up to. Higher temperatures tend to cause heat exhaustion or heat stroke (see chapter 4). And since cavies do not take kindly to great temperature changes, avoid wide fluctuations: a constant 60 degrees, or even 55 degrees, is preferable, for instance, to the conditions found in an unheated garage, where temperatures may reach 80 degrees Fahrenheit or higher during the day and drop to 40 degrees at night, lower in winter.

Whatever the temperature of your cavy's home, good ventilation is a must. Without proper ventilation, especially when you have a number of cavy cages, the air can become humid, stagnant, and heavy with the odor of ammonia (a major component of urine). While providing good ventilation, you must also be sure to prevent drafts. The solution? Use an exhaust fan rather than one that blows cool air into the room.

In warmer weather, it's possible to house your cavy

outdoors. Begin on a warm spring day. Put your cavy outside, making sure that he's safe from rain, direct sunlight, drafts, and wandering cats and dogs. At first, take him inside during the cool nights. Then slowly lengthen the time spent outdoors until your cavy is outside around the clock. Some breeders even allow their guinea pigs to graze, providing a movable fence and ground boxes for shelter. But cavies should never be allowed to graze in grasses treated with insecticides or herbicides.

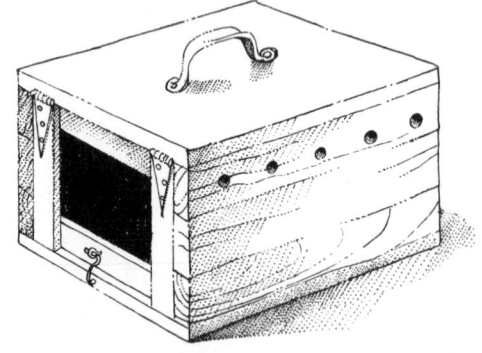

You may want to bore holes in both sides of the carrying case for added ventilation.

ON THE ROAD

It may be a good idea to have a special traveling home for your cavy—a closed box with plenty of ventilation that can be decorated as you wish. This is a much safer temporary home for your pet than tiny boxes, shoes, or even purses and pockets. A carrying case will help to make sure that the guinea pig isn't accidentally dropped as he is transported from one place to another, even if it's only across the room.

3
WHAT TO EAT

Your cavy needs more than a warm, dry, well-ventilated place to come home to, of course. He'll also have to be fed—and proper feeding for the cavy can be as simple or as fancy as you want to make it. Basically, a cavy needs only cavy pellets and water. All the other tidbits you give him are treats, unless pellets are not available and you need to feed your pet a mixture of grains instead. If you keep this in mind, you'll have a happy and healthy guinea pig. Too much of anything except pellets, water, and hay can cause problems such as vitamin deficiencies and diarrhea (see chapter 4).

Cavies require cool, fresh water at all times. The best kind of dispenser, which can be bought at a pet shop, is a plastic water bottle with a tube at the end of a stopper. Some tubes have a small ball at the end that limits the amount of water dripped when your cavy plays with the nozzle (something he'll do quite often). Water crocks, which are weighted at the bottom to prevent tipping, are also acceptable dispensers, but these must be thoroughly cleaned more often since cavies see nothing wrong with putting themselves, shavings, food, and droppings into the water. Bottles should be emptied and cleaned with a bottle brush daily, while water in a crock needs to be changed twice a day. The bottle and the crock should be washed as any of your own dishes are washed, with warm water and soap, making sure that no soapy residue is left behind.

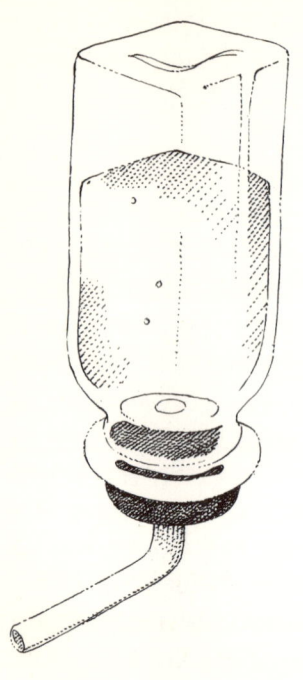

A cavy water dispenser should hold about sixteen ounces of fluid.

Pellets should be supplied "free choice," meaning you just leave plenty of them in a heavy, untippable dish in the cage and let the cavies eat at their leisure. Commercially prepared guinea pig pellets are more expensive than other chows, but they do contain the correct proportion of all the nutrients important for good guinea pig health and growth. Rabbit pellets may be fed to cavies, but this particular chow doesn't contain the vitamin C supplement that cavies need because they cannot manufacture their own, as other rodents do. So if you use rabbit chow for your cavy—or if you use a mixture of grains instead of pellets—you'll have to supply him with other sources of vitamin C: orange rind or pulp, lettuce, dandelion greens, grasses, potato skins, or one teaspoon of orange juice in the drinking water each day. You can also supplement with one or two drops of pediatric liquid vitamin C, which you can buy at your local drugstore. You feed these directly into the cavy's mouth so you know exactly how much the animal is getting.

A combination of oats, soy, corn, and wheat is a suitable substitute for pellets as the cavy's main diet. Oats and soybeans are high in protein, which is important for good muscle tone. Corn provides carbohydrates essential for making fat, which the animal draws upon for body warmth and energy. Because of this, the amount of corn fed should be increased in cold weather and decreased in warm weather if the animals are kept in a barn, cool cellar, or garage. The oils and vitamins of wheat seem to improve the cavy's coat sheen and breeding vitality. Hulled sunflower seeds are also a good source of oils and vitamins needed for bright coat sheen and good health. It is hard to determine an exact proportion that is suitable for each feeding situation. Begin with 50 percent oats and add the other grains to make up the difference. Then experiment to find the diet best for your cavy. A few breeders feed their cavies only horse-sweet feed, which is a mixture of oats, corn, bran mixed with molasses, and vitamin C.

Cavies on a grain-mixture or rabbit-pellet diet will also need greens and grasses, fruits and vegetables, to get enough vitamins. However, these foods should be introduced in small amounts, so that a tolerance can be built up. Too many greens can cause diarrhea, dehydration, and death within a very few days. If you slowly but steadily increase your guinea pigs' intake of greens, they will eventually be able to live totally on vegetables and grass in the summertime. Begin with a quarter of a medium-sized lettuce leaf each day, along with the pellets or grain, and build up from there. Just remember that a young cavy's favorite food may be lettuce and he will easily overeat and make himself sick. Above all, make sure that any greens that go into your cavy's cage are crisp and clean: any wilt or black spots can cause diarrhea. And, of course, never feed your guinea pig any grass or dandelions that have been chemically treated.

Cavies love hay, a good choice for a grass and an excellent feed supplement—with the added attraction that it provides an extra absorbent layer over the bedding in your pet's cage. Running and jumping through this lush green is a popular cavy pastime that shines his coat at the same time. Hay (or alfalfa cubes) bought in small bags from pet shops, supermarkets, or dime stores is usually free of thorns and prickly weeds. Hay purchased by the bale from a nearby farm should be carefully searched for thorns and thistles since, if they lodge in the cavy's mouth or throat, they can cause abrasions and infections.

Hay provides added nutrition, dry bedding, and entertainment.

Besides vegetables and grasses, usually thought of as the cavy's favorite foods, consider milksops—bread crusts soaked in room-temperature milk. Cavies also love such breakfast leftovers as cereal, milk, toast, and oranges. Yes, it's all right to feed your cavy a variety of "people" food, though very few guinea pigs are partial to tomatoes, potatoes, cauliflower, onions, and meat. But it can't be stated strongly enough that the best way to make sure that your pet is getting a balanced diet is to feed him commercial pellets or a grain mixture, grasses such as hay, and vitamin C, limiting all other foods to "treats."

One last note on feeding. The vitamin C supplement in guinea pig pellets will last only for about thirty days in hot weather and ninety days in cold. After this time, the vitamin C is gone and you're actually feeding rabbit pellets to your cavy while paying for the more expensive guinea pig chow. Your pets may start to show signs of scurvy (see chapter 4) if you are not careful. So, when buying guinea pig pellets, remember that the small boxes of food sitting on the dime store or supermarket shelf may have been there a very long time. Try to make sure that the feed is relatively fresh. Buy from a store where you know that there is a reasonably fast turnover, for example, a pet shop that sells cavies, a farm and home center, or a feed store. Most important, do not buy more feed than you can use in thirty days. Store it in a cool, dry place and discard any that appears old or moldy.

Feeding your cavy well is easy to do if you keep fresh water and feed (pellets or grains) in his home at all times, provide hay or alfalfa cubes if possible, and give him snacks as treats or rewards. *Your* reward will be a happy, well-fed guinea pig.

4
KEEPING OR GETTING YOUR PIG IN THE PINK

An apple a day keeps the doctor away. An ounce of prevention is worth a pound of cure. Old sayings, but still true. For guinea pigs, too, the best treatment is preventive medicine.

Keep your cavy's cage clean and dry. Make sure it gets good ventilation and lots of light, and that the temperature remains fairly constant at about 65 to 70 degrees Fahrenheit. Provide your cavy with fresh, properly balanced food and with fresh, cool water. These are the basic ingredients for a strong and healthy cavy. There are no yearly vaccinations, and routine veterinary checkups are unnecessary unless there is an obvious problem.

Take precautions when moving any guinea pig. To lift your cavy properly, place one hand over its neck and around its shoulders. With the other hand, gently reach under the belly and rump to support the body as you lift. It is safe to carry your pet this way—with one hand under him and the other over the top of him. You can also bring him in close to your body with his feet and stomach resting against your shoulder or chest. If he is facing toward you, you can easily use this method to pick him up and to turn him on his back to examine his underside. Don't worry about overhandling or overholding your cavy as long as you are careful and gentle. Cavies love being loved, and cuddling them is one way of showing them that you do.

Hold the cavy gently but firmly when lifting.

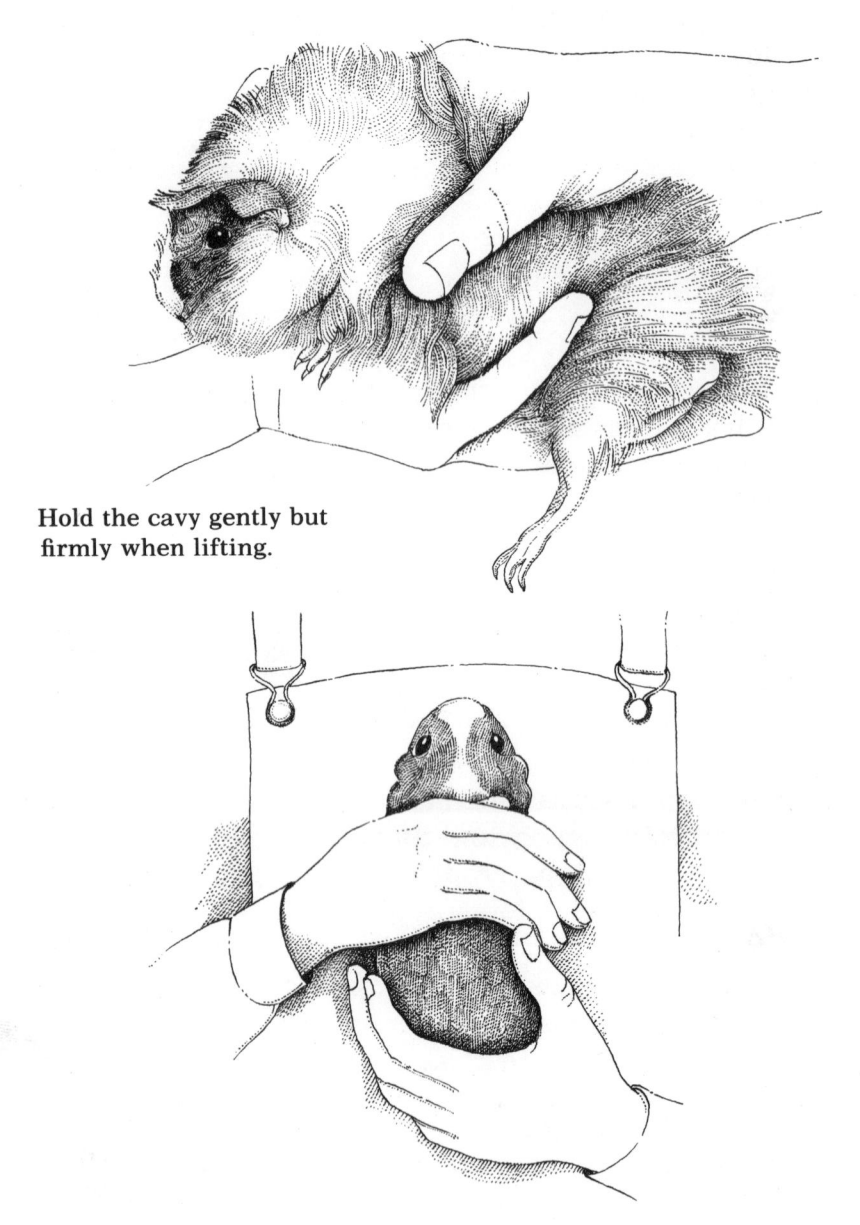

To make sure your cavy feels secure and to prevent wiggling, support the animal's bottom and back whenever he is carried.

Moving a guinea pig from one home to another can mean problems, especially for cavies over two years of age. The stress involved in a big change of scene can disturb the balance in a cavy's system and increase the chance of illness. (A prime example is the class pet that's taken home for vacation and never makes it back to class.) Another big change is getting a new pet. Never suddenly introduce a new guinea pig to your guinea pig household: keep the newcomer by himself for a while (at least a week) as a period of adjustment or, if he does become ill, as quarantine. And, whenever possible, try not to make any major changes in the environment of your cavy—especially as he gets older and less able to adapt to new surroundings and changes in water or feeding. If you take your pet to a cavy show or on vacation to Grandma's, take along some of the food and a bottle of water from home. Mix a little of these with a little of the food and water from the new area, gradually increasing the new and decreasing the old. This is not to say that your cavy will always become ill when you change its settings, only that sickness is more likely during these times.

WHAT TO DO UNTIL THE DOCTOR COMES

Even with the best prevention and precautions, illnesses and accidents do occur. All too frequently treatment of unwell cavies can be extremely difficult, especially since cavies are not complainers, and the symptoms of their disorders are often far from obvious. Sometimes, in fact, the first inkling you have of an ailment is when you find a guinea pig dead in its cage.

So you'll want to watch your cavies closely. Be aware of specific cavy-illness symptoms, which are described below, and the most common general ones: lack of appetite and listlessness. If your guinea pig isn't eating or drinking as usual, it's likely that something is wrong.

What can you do when you suspect that your pet is sick or wounded? First of all, isolate him. Don't just put him in a cage or cardboard carton by himself: remove him from the room where other cavies live, since some diseases are infectious and can be transmitted through the air from cage to cage. You needn't worry about yourself or other family members—in most cases there is little danger of humans contracting cavy diseases. If you are at all concerned, check with your veterinarian. Next, try to keep your cavy eating. Offer him his favorite foods. Encourage him to keep munching and drinking, because a day or two without food or water will lead to dehydration. Since the largest part of the body's cells is taken up by water, dehydration is sure to increase the seriousness of any ailment. A little eating and drinking may help to prevent the "nose in the corner" syndrome, which happens when an ill cavy turns his face toward a corner of the cage, hunches up, and simply sits there until he dies.

As soon as you realize that your cavy needs treatment, check with a veterinarian. Many years of college and experience have made the animal doctor the one best able to help your pet get better. For the location of a good vet, or the one nearest you, check with your neighbors or look in the Yellow Pages of your phone book under ANIMAL HOSPITALS. If the vet can't advise you —some deal mostly with larger animals—he or she may refer you to one with more interest and knowledge in the field, or to an experienced cavy breeder in your area. If you must carry your pet any distance, make sure he is transported in a warm, draft-free box or carrying case.

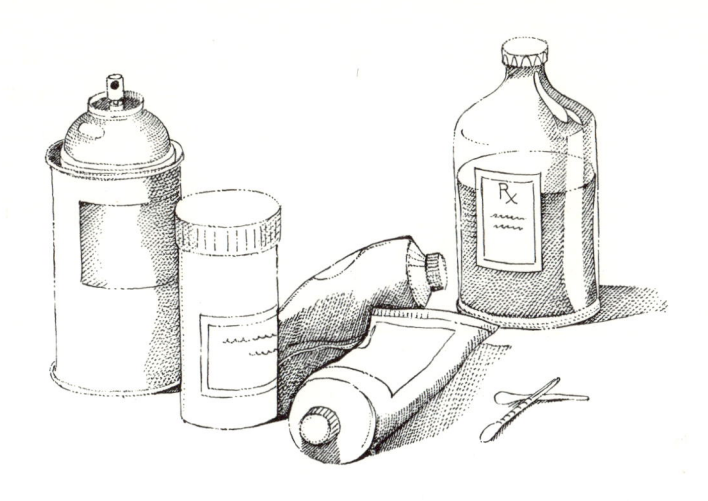

YOUR CAVY'S MEDICINE CHEST

Here's a list of basic medications to have on hand for cavy emergencies. Most drugs are described by their generic names, which may differ from manufacturers' brand names. Most are easily obtainable from either a pharmacy or a veterinary hospital. Remember: all medications should be kept safely locked away from small children. While none of these drugs would be extremely harmful to humans if swallowed, they could make a person very sick to his or her stomach.

- All-purpose antibiotic or a sulfa drug, to combat systemic bacterial infections. All antibiotics, such as chloramphenicol, should be used with great care since overdosing can cause diarrhea. A sulfa drug, such as sulfamethazine 12.5 percent solution, is, on the other hand, extremely safe since there are few side effects. Use one teaspoon (five cc.) of sulfamethazine per one cup (eight ounces) water. Continue using it until the symptoms have been gone for at least three days.

- Antibacterial eyewash or drops, such as neomycin sulfate ophthalmic drops or ointment, for eye infections or wounds. Other ophthalmic solutions are safe, too, but be sure there are no steroids in them. Steroids aggravate open wounds.
- Antibacterial wound ointment, such as mycitracin or bacitracin. You can use other drugs, too, as long as they do not contain steroids such as cortisone. Cortisone will further irritate the wound and delay healing.
- Cat or small-animal flea and lice powder or spray. Anything good for a cat is usually good for cavies. The spray or powder will keep down the external parasite problems caused by lice and mites, common in guinea pigs.
- Diarrhea medication. Biosol (neomycin sulfate) is a good one, but be very careful with it since you can easily stop up a cavy totally with it. Kaopectate is a much safer drug. Use one-quarter teaspoon (1.25 cc.) directly into the mouth three to four times a day. Cut back the dosage as soon as the diarrhea symptoms begin to disappear.
- One-cubic-centimeter (cc.) syringes are good for measuring medication and can also be used as nursers for orphaned or weak youngsters.
- Cotton balls and cotton-tipped applicators are useful for cleaning wounds and infections.
- Rubbing alcohol is good to have on hand to wash out wounds and infections.

AND . . . TWO REMINDERS

1. *Never* use penicillin with cavies. It is likely to harm them. Other antibiotics are also dangerous; they kill both beneficial as well as harmful bacteria. Diarrhea can result from an overdose of certain antibiotics,

which can weaken your cavy's resistance and make him more susceptible to other diseases.

2. Remember the rules for *preventing* cavy ailments and you may never have to use anything at all!

GUINEA PIG AILMENTS AND HOW TO TREAT THEM

ABSCESSES — In guinea pigs, abscesses most often appear as lumps, or hard, round nodules, around the throat, face, and ears. These bacterial infections are usually noticed after the cavy has been under stress or has come in contact with abrasive material—hay containing thorns, for example. They can also be caused by a bacterial infection that may have begun somewhere else in the body. (Abscesses on the body are less common and are generally the result of infected bites or other injuries.) Sometimes they can get as large as golf balls. If left untreated, the natural development of the abscess is to grow until a soft spot eventually forms. Then the cavy will scratch until he opens the lump,

Abscesses commonly appear on the cavy's neck and throat.

causing the pus inside it to drain. By adding sulfamethazine to your cavy's water, using a proportion of five cc. (one teaspoon) of the medicine to eight ounces (one cup) water, you may retard the natural development of the abscess. If the abscess is in an advanced stage, a veterinarian may lance it with a scalpel blade, drain out the pus, and apply a mild antiseptic to the wound. Once the abscess is opened—whether by the cavy's scratching it or by outside attention—it usually disappears within a few days. An unopened abscess, however, may remain for several weeks before it opens naturally or is reabsorbed.

New cavy owners sometimes become unnecessarily alarmed by abscesses, mistaking the lumps of pus for tumors. Tumors, happily, are rare in guinea pigs; when they do occur, they appear as solid lumps, most often in the mammary glands.

BROKEN BONES — Cavies may suffer broken legs and toes from falling, running on wire, or being dropped. Their little bones are so delicate that you can usually assume there is a break if the pet is using only three legs. Breaks can be splinted or pinned by a veterinarian. But most simple fractures can heal equally well—in about six weeks—if you isolate the injured cavy in a small area, with just enough room for him to move around. And make sure there's food and water close by at all times.

COCCIDIOSIS — This is a relatively uncommon infectious disease caused by microscopic parasites called coccidia. Cavies can pick up these protozoa by eating infected food or bedding. The symptoms of the illness are listlessness, loss of appetite, and diarrhea. Since coccidiosis is highly contagious, the sick cavy should be isolated and his cage should be thoroughly scrubbed.

If diagnosed early enough by your vet, coccidiosis is rarely fatal. The pet doctor will give you Biosol or a similar drug, one or two drops of which should be placed directly into the mouth two or three times a day until the diarrhea disappears.

Coccidiosis can usually be prevented by regular and thorough cage cleaning. Since it takes the protozoa from eight to twelve days after their arrival to form the disease-causing spores, diligent cleaning can generally be counted on to interrupt this spore-forming process.

COLDS — Cavies catch colds, or more precisely bacterial and viral infections, easily. As with humans, cold symptoms include wheezes, sneezes, coughs, and runny noses. In all cases, the sick cavy should be isolated.

If your cavy's respiratory infection is caused by a virus (viral pneumonia, for example), nothing can be done to control the infection. But you *can* do your best to make your new pet as comfortable as possible. Above all, you'll want to help your cavy breathe more easily. You can do this by dabbing a decongestant ointment—like Vick's Vaporub, for instance—on the paws and above the nostrils. (The cavy will keep renewing the treatment each time he rubs his nose with his paw.) Or you can dunk a cotton ball in oil of eucalyptus (available at drugstores and pet shops), place the cotton in the cage, and cover the cage with a large towel.

Infections caused by bacteria, however, can be treated. The most common types—bordetella bronchiseptica and streptococci pneumonia—will usually respond to sulfamethazine; use one teaspoon (five cc.) per one cup (eight ounces) water. A veterinarian may be able to prescribe an antibiotic especially developed to combat the particular infection-causing bacteria—chloramphenicol, for example—by taking a culture from your cavy's runny nose to find out which kind of bacterium your cavy is fighting.

DIARRHEA — This is the ailment you're most likely to encounter with your cavy. It may even cause death, especially in the young guinea pig. The cavy's problems with excretion, which are caused by inflammation of the intestines, can lead to dehydration and prove fatal as soon as forty-eight hours after the first appearance of the condition.

Because of the seriousness of this disorder, you'll want to prevent your cavy from developing diarrhea if you possibly can. Some causes of intestinal inflammation are difficult to fight against—viral infections, for example—but you *can* decrease the chances of diarrhea with regular cage cleaning and with careful attention to your cavy's eating habits and environment. For instance, don't give a guinea pig, especially a young one, too many different kinds of new food all at once. And remember to avoid changing your cavy's habitat, diet, and water supply too suddenly. Watch out for diarrhea in your cavy—a loose or watery stool—and act quickly if it appears. Isolate the animal and give him nothing to eat or drink except pellets and fresh-boiled water, cooled to room temperature. A mixture of cooled boiled milk and water (half of each) can be provided instead of just the water. This mixture should not be allowed to stand around, but should be changed several times each day. If diarrhea continues after twenty-four hours, call your veterinarian: he or she may prescribe Biosol or some other antidiarrhetic. These medications must be used with care to avoid causing constipation. Depending upon the size of your pet, give him two to three drops directly in his mouth three times each day until the diarrhea symptoms begin to disappear. Then taper down the dose to once a day for two days. Diarrhea is a highly dangerous ailment, but one that can be cured with early treatment.

EAR PROBLEMS — Cavies occasionally develop an infection of the middle or inner ear that causes them to hold their heads to one side. Sometimes their sense of balance is also affected. Some breeders and veterinarians believe this to be a virtually untreatable condition. It is impossible to determine whether the invading organisms are bacteria or viruses; therefore a veterinarian will usually prescribe an antibiotic that will destroy harmful bacteria. An infected cavy moves in an awkward manner, with his head tilted and sometimes with one leg extended forward. He may fall over on his side, flailing his legs helplessly in an effort to right himself. The problem does not seem to be contagious to other cagemates. Nor does an antibiotic seem to have any effect on the viral form of this disease. With or without treatment, it runs its own course. Although it is rarely fatal, it often leaves the cavy with a slight head tilt.

EYE PROBLEMS — Conjunctivitis is an inflammation of the membrane covering the front part of the eyeball and the inner surface of the eyelid. If your cavy has conjunctivitis, the white part of the eye will appear pink and the area around the eyelid will be noticeably inflamed. The condition may be caused by irritation (as from dust, shavings, or hay) or by infection (from a virus or bacteria). If an organism is the cause of the infection, the disease may be highly contagious to other cavies and even, possibly, to humans (check with your veterinarian). In such cases, strict isolation of the sick cavy is a requirement.

Whatever the cause, conjunctivitis should be treated with an ophthalmic solution or ointment—neomycin sulfate or mycitracin, for example. When applied directly to the eyes—something very easy to do—several times a day, the medication will kill bacteria, lubricate the eye, and reduce inflammation.

Cloudiness sometimes appears in the eyes of newborns, youngsters, or injured cavies. This opacity in young cavies usually disappears within a week without treatment, though an ophthalmic solution will help to speed the clearing process. (If an infant cavy's cloudiness does not disappear, congenital cataracts may be present, and the blind cavy should be put to sleep.) When cloudiness is caused by a cornea injury (due to a fight or abrasive bedding), the best treatment again is an ophthalmic solution administered several times a day.

FUNGUS — Different kinds of fungus can cause infection in both animals and humans. Ringworm is a good ex-

External parasites can cause bald patches in a cavy coat.

ample. Ringworm is not a worm at all but a tiny microscopic plant that, though fairly uncommon, sometimes attaches itself to guinea pigs (as well as to dogs, cats, and people) and grows. You will know if this is happening to your pet if circular bare spots show up on the abdomen or back. If the infection is a small one, you can apply an antifungal ointment containing griseofulvin, which is available from a drugstore without a prescription, to the affected areas. When the infection is widespread, however, you will need griseofulvin in its oral form, which requires a prescription from a veterinarian.

Other fungal infections occasionally affect guinea pigs. Eating moldy hay or pellets (mold is a fungus) can sometimes cause internal infections that may lead to inflammation of the intestines and diarrhea. Some molds are extremely toxic and any food found to have mold should be discarded.

HAIR LOSS — When a cavy seems to be losing his hair, there are several possible causes:
- *Allergies.* Some cavies have an allergic reaction to cedar shavings, which are often used as bedding. If the cedar is the cause, substituting pine shavings should return hair to normal within a few weeks. Check to see if anything new has recently been added to your pet's environment. Any new object or food might be the cause of hair loss.
- *Chewing.* Some cavies, especially those on a diet without hay, will chew on their own coats or those of their cagemates. Since this chewing may also be caused by boredom, try to introduce playthings into the cage—cardboard boxes,

empty toilet-paper rolls, and hanging paper balls —to divert your cavies' attention. Then, chewing will most likely decrease.
- *Vitamin Deficiencies.* A lack of nutrients, especially vitamin C, can cause hair loss—most often in pregnant sows, whose diet is being shared with unborn cavies. In such cases, provide the deficient cavy with extra greens or add water-soluble vitamin C to the drinking water. Sows treated this way usually have regrown their coats by the time their youngsters are weaned. Other cavies may suffer deficiencies if they are fed food that has been sitting on the store shelf for a long time. Remember, use only the freshest food for your pets—they deserve quality.
- *Parasites.* See LICE AND MITES.

HEAT REACTION — Cavies are unusually sensitive to heat —and severe reactions, even deaths, are not uncommon. Heavily pregnant sows are especially prone to heat exhaustion or sunstroke. So, always protect guinea pigs from direct sunlight. Never put your cavy's cage near an open window on a warm, sunny day, and remember to provide good ventilation. Be careful when transporting cavies in automobiles: the lack of air circulation can be fatal.

Symptoms of heat reaction include drooling and weakness. A cavy so affected should be immediately placed in the shade and wiped down (especially around the face, ears, and feet) with a cool, wet cloth.

IMPACTION — A large block of feces near the cavy's anal opening or elsewhere within the large intestine is a fairly common condition, usually found in older boars (two years or more). If your cavy gives off an unpleasant odor, inspect the anal area. Clean out whatever blockage is found there by gently grasping it with a tissue or damp paper towel. Adding extra greens to the cavy's diet may ease this problem and, since most cavies are able to get rid of their own wastes around the impaction, the condition is usually more a nuisance than a serious danger.

LICE AND MITES — These tiny bugs, so small that they can't be seen easily by the naked eye, can be a sizable cavy problem. Sometimes called "creeping dandruff," lice and mites live on guinea pigs and cause great discomfort. If your cavy is scratching bare spots in his coat, these parasites are the likely culprits. Look for a whitish or blackish residue deep in the coat or on the ends of the hairs. To combat the problem, dust your cavies with cat or small-animal flea and lice powder every two weeks. Lice and mites are cavy problems, not people problems. They will not infest you.

PREGNANCY PROBLEMS — See chapter 5.

SCURVY — If your cavy walks with his hind end tucked down, if he squeals from pain when touched, if he's losing his hair and his muscle tone, he probably has scurvy—a disease caused by a vitamin C deficiency. The most common reason? Cavy owners forget that feed pellets that did contain vitamin C when purchased lose their vitamin C over time—thirty days in warm weather, about ninety days in cold. To prevent scurvy in your pet, use only fresh pellets and supplement your cavy's diet with greens and other tidbits rich in vitamin C. If pellets are not available in your area or if the price

The best treatment for scurvy is liquid vitamin C fed through a dropper.

is too high, feed grain foods and the vitamin C supplement. If your cavy does develop scurvy, even a severe case can usually be corrected in a few weeks with pediatric vitamin C drops administered directly into the cavy's mouth. The drops are sold at all pharmacies and are usually stocked in the baby supplies section. One or two drops a day will do fine.

TEETH PROBLEMS — Cavy teeth grow throughout the animal's lifetime. So broken teeth—which may result from a fall or from biting cage bars—are not a very serious problem. While the damaged teeth are repairing themselves, simply provide ground-up pellets, cornmeal, farina, oatmeal, and other soft foods. If the teeth are uneven or overly long, they can easily be clipped with a pair of human toenail clippers. It is *very* easy to do and doesn't hurt the animal *at all*. Don't worry!

A far more severe problem occurs when molars, the back teeth, grow in improperly—out of alignment—and do not wear down evenly. If this condition continues unchecked, the teeth will grow over the tongue, trapping it, sometimes causing starvation. Keep a close eye on your cavy's teeth, and watch for drooling as a possible symptom of improper alignment. If noticed in time, a veterinarian can correct the situation by filing down the teeth.

WEAKNESS (WASTING DISEASE) — Sometimes a cavy becomes progressively weaker, more debilitated, and more off-balance—whether because of a virus, nerve damage suffered by sows during delivery (see chapter 5), or vitamin deficiency. The condition is first noticeable at the hind end, as the cavy tucks his rear end under or hunches his back and hops along, dragging his two hind feet. Untreated, this condition becomes "wasting disease," which is a general term used to describe extreme weight loss, and leads to death. (Some cases of wasting disease, however, may well be cases of starvation due to overgrown molars. See TEETH PROBLEMS.) If a vitamin deficiency is the cause, the disease can be treated by supplying additional greens, wheat germ, and other vitamin sources. Otherwise all you can do is to try to keep your cavy eating and drinking—it may even be necessary to hand-feed him. Unfortunately, complete recovery is rare and takes many weeks to achieve.

WOUNDS — Most cavy wounds—including torn toenails or toes—are satisfactorily treated by a thorough cleaning (with warm water) and a light application of a mild antiseptic or antibacterial ointment, such as mycitracin or bacitracin. Stronger antiseptics should be avoided because guinea pigs tend to lick themselves, and if they ingest whatever you're applying, it may be poisonous to them.

WHAT TO DO WHEN AN ANIMAL DIES

For whatever reason, if one of your guinea pigs does die, thoroughly disinfect the cage. If the cage is made of wood, wash, rinse, scrape, sand, and revarnish it; then allow it to air in the sun. In order to help to protect your surviving guinea pigs, have a veterinarian examine the dead cavy. This postmortem can often identify the cause of a dangerous infection and determine what drugs can be used to treat the survivors. Even better, the postmortem may prove that the cause of death was *not* infectious, in which case there's no danger to the rest of your herd.

With good care and proper treatment in times of illness, your cavy can live to a ripe old age. Our oldest guinea pig lived a productive eight years. Usually, you can expect the average pet to live four to five years. But even with the best of care, the inevitable must one day occur.

Our Princess died first, and then Toastie. They were our first guinea pigs, and although they were "needle noses," they were quality cavies in our eyes. Princess and Toastie were old pigs, seven and eight years old, but they did tricks, they called us, and they were our friends. We were sad when Princess died, healthy, in her sleep. The whole family mourned. We got a shoebox and gently placed her in it, bedded down in sweet-smelling hay. We dug a deep hole in the back field and put her to rest there. The children cried and I cried too.

Then Princess's daughter, Toastie, got sick. We nursed her for a long time. Sometimes it looked as if she might get better—she was such a strong animal. Eventually, though, we realized that Toastie was not going to recover: her breath was difficult for her to draw and we couldn't hand-feed her anymore. We thought about taking her to our veterinarian to be put to sleep, but since she didn't seem to be suffering, only in a deep sleep, we decided to have her spend her last hours at home with us. So we all sat around helplessly and waited for her to take her last breath. When it came, we buried our pet beside her mom. It was a sad occasion, but we all felt relief that Toastie was no longer struggling. Losing a pet that you have tended and loved is not easy. It hurts. But wonderful memories of the good times and the funny things that happened live on. You will always feel the love for your pet and the love he felt for you.

A new pet can never take the place of the old one, but it can fill an empty space left by your lost friend. And a new guinea pig can be fun in some of the same ways and some different ones, just because of its different personality or colors. You can be loyal to your old cavy and still love your new one. Give it a try . . . keep on cavying!

5
TO BREED OR NOT TO BREED: PROBLEMS AND REWARDS

Birth and babies are exciting, appealing ideas, so almost any guinea pig owner will probably want to set off on the adventure of breeding. However, before taking that first big step of putting Big George together with your Lonesome Lila, think carefully about the fact that there is some risk in every pregnancy. And this risk increases considerably when the sow is more than a year old: in fact, an older sow, one that hasn't been a mother before, has little chance of surviving her first litter. When the sow delivers her young, the pelvic bones—those through which the baby must pass in order to be born—actually separate to allow very large babies to pass through. If the female is allowed to mature fully, to one year of age, before becoming pregnant, these bones will fuse, and future pregnancies will end in death for both the sow and the fetuses when the babies become entrapped by the bones. So think about it. Do you want to take the chance of losing the sow? How upset would you be if both the sow and the litter died in a difficult delivery?

A more cheerful but equally serious question is: What will you do with all the infant cavies that may arrive with a normal delivery? Since the sow may produce more than one egg and the boar may fertilize more than one, there could be as many as seven babies in a litter. If you can't keep them all yourself, will you be able to find other homes for them? And will you be able to part with them when the time comes?

Consider all these questions, and if breeding cavies still seems right and exciting for you, dive right in. Most pregnancies and deliveries are normal, smooth, and easy. Most experiences with breeding are full of wonder, excitement, and fun.

SETTING THE SCENE

It takes two to tango—and to have babies. For the best, healthiest breeding, both the sow and the boar should be four to six months old, each weighing at least one and a half pounds. Younger sows and boars should be kept in separate cages and should not be allowed to breed until they are older: a very young sow (three weeks or older) *can* get pregnant, but she usually won't be able to carry her babies full term (about sixty-three days) and deliver a normal, fully developed baby. If the boar is too large—three to four pounds, for example—the resulting fetus may be overly large, causing problems for the sow in delivery.

When you have a sow and boar that meet the breeding requirements—about one and a half pounds each, four to six months old—put them in a cage together and let nature take its course. In other words, just watch and wait—conception will happen without your help. It is not necessary to have two animals of the same breed (American, Abyssinian, and so on), but if you don't, the resulting offspring will be mongrels, just like a collie/shepherd-crossed puppy would be. (For more information on this topic, see chapter 6.) If your cage is a large one (twenty-four inches by twenty-four inches, for instance), a second sow of the right size and age for breeding can also share the "love nest." One boar can easily handle the breeding for four to six sows as long as the animals are not overcrowded.

Breeding usually takes place at night, although the boar can often be seen chasing the sows during the day. Mark your calendar on the day that you first put sow and boar together, and you can expect a litter some sixty-three to seventy days (nine weeks) later, depending upon the timing of the sow's estrous cycle. This cycle, the time it takes her ovaries to produce eggs and release them into the tubes of her uterus, where each can be fertilized by only one of the male's millions of sperm, lasts about seventeen days. She may become pregnant immediately after mating, or it may take a week or two of breeding for conception to occur. Since the gestation period, the time between conception and birth, is approximately sixty-three days, using sixty-three to seventy days as a guide for estimating a delivery date allows for differences in the estrous cycle.

During the sow's nine weeks of pregnancy, you'll want to take extra-special care of her. Since she needs lots of vitamins C and D, try feeding her lettuce, bread milksops, and cereals in addition to her normal diet. It is often difficult for the novice breeder to tell when a sow has conceived. Her profile doesn't usually begin to bulge in an obvious way until she is at least halfway through her pregnancy. And her personality doesn't change until about one week before she delivers. If she is carrying only a single fetus, you may not know she is pregnant until you find the youngster nursing one morning.

Occasionally a heavily pregnant sow will lose hair and develop cracked skin on her abdomen or underarms. Sometimes this is due to a vitamin deficiency and can be controlled by increasing her intake of substances rich in vitamins and oils, such as wheat germ oil. Whatever the cause (hormone changes and stretching skin may also be responsible), much of the sow's discomfort can be relieved by applying baby oil to the irritated areas.

Make sure the future mom has plenty of room for exercise right up until the time of delivery. And, as delivery time draws nearer, avoid handling or carrying her. If you *must* lift the pregnant sow, keep one hand beneath her heavy rear end for support and lift with a gentle scooping motion. Always be gentle, and try to limit the sow's straining and struggling as you lift her. Any stress or upset at this delicate time may contribute to pregnancy problems, such as toxemia.

From the time of conception, changes occur in the

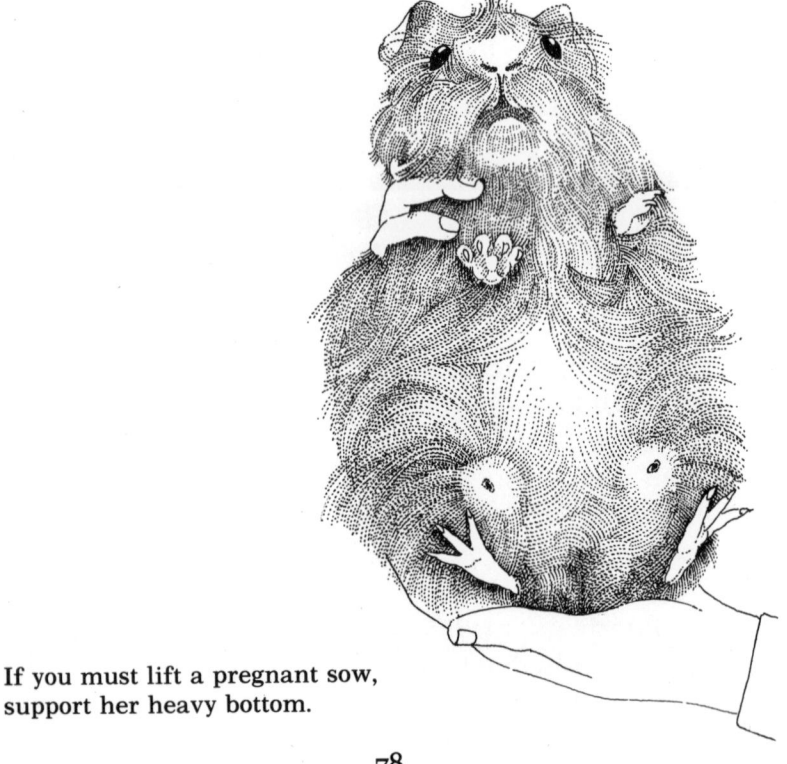

If you must lift a pregnant sow, support her heavy bottom.

sow's body. The two horns or tubes of her uterus and the blood vessels that lead to and from it become enlarged. This organ and the surrounding blood vessels will safely hold and nurture the developing babies, which grow along the two tubes like peas in a pod. Some veterinarians have observed that babies usually develop in one tube or the other, varying from pregnancy to pregnancy. Over a period of nine weeks there is a great change from single-celled eggs into beautiful baby cavies. Every day is important in their unborn lives. By the time they are three- to four-week-old fetuses, the dividing, differentiating, growing cells of the original eggs have developed little bodies, heads, legs, eyes, noses, and mouths, although they are still very, very tiny. Each receives food and oxygen from the placenta, which is attached to the wall of the uterus, through an umbilical cord. Wastes from the fetus are also carried away through the umbilical cord. Surrounded by warm amniotic fluid, the developing babies are cushioned from the bumps of the outside world. The last four weeks before birth are spent growing stronger and maturing.

It is after the first month that you can detect a change in the mom. As the fetuses grow, her uterus stretches, as does her skin. Her abdomen begins to bulge just a little, then a little more. At the end of her term, she looks like a little blimp. She often appears to have a tiny head and shoulders, and a huge flattened, balloon-shaped body. It's frequently an effort for her to get to food and water. At this time, make her life as easy as possible by putting her food dish and water close by.

Pregnancies in cavies can be smooth and uncomplicated. This is usually the case. However, they can also be difficult and dangerous. If problems arise, don't

One month into pregnancy, a sow's body begins to widen.

hesitate to get help! Call your veterinarian! Even with a veterinarian's help, though, many problem pregnancies, for no apparent reason, end in the death of the sow and her litter. Despite the best of care, a pregnant sow, especially an older one, may become lethargic, give up eating and drinking, and die. This unexplained death is usually termed pregnancy toxemia.

Unlike some animals, cavies don't make nests, but the sow may create a warm, special place for the birth of her litter. A week or more before delivery, she may choose her spot in the cage, sit there, and stare out dreamily for long periods of time. As she stares, the sow will turn her body from side to side, making herself more comfortable: this turning eventually creates a hollow in the cage bedding—a kind of nest for the cavy birth.

In the last few days before delivery, the sow may begin to eat less, sitting and staring off into space more and more, shifting her weight, trying to make her bulky body comfortable. This is the time to remove the boar, since he will rebreed the sow immediately after the delivery—both events surely wearing out the sow.

During this last stage of her pregnancy, the ligaments holding her pelvic muscles relax. This allows the pelvic bones to separate enough to let the relatively huge babies pass through. A few hours before labor begins, she may become restless, busily cleaning droppings and other debris away from her chosen spot.

BIRTH OF A CAVY OR LOTS OF CAVIES

When zero hour arrives, the sow will rise up on her toes and push out from her pelvic area. As her contractions get stronger, she may squeal a little or grunt, her ears rising in time with the contractions. The first baby should arrive within fifteen to twenty minutes after hard labor has begun. The sow will reach between her hind legs and, making the weirdest contortions, gently grab onto her baby with her teeth and pull him out. (Sometimes the baby emerges nose first, sometimes rear end first.) The baby usually slides out easily because he is covered with the slippery birth sac. Once the two- to four-ounce baby is out, the mother nips open the sac and cuts the umbilical cord with her teeth. The newborn cavy will usually give a few little coughs, as the sow continues cleaning and warming the baby by licking and tucking him beneath her body. She'll also eat the umbilical cord, the birth sac, and the placenta —a thorough clean-up operation that also includes eating some of the cage bedding. This is very remarkable when you consider the fact that at all other times the cavy is a vegetarian.

This first baby may be the sow's only delivery. But there may well be as many as six more to come. After the first delivery, contractions may begin again very quickly, or they may begin after more than twenty minutes have passed. There is no cause for worry as long as the sow is busily occupied with her brood and does not appear to be distressed. However much time it takes, under normal circumstances the mother will repeat the birth and cleaning process with each baby.

PROBLEMS TO WATCH FOR

Usually the sow can manage her own deliveries without help. But sometimes delivery problems, called dystocia, do occur. If your sow appears to be in distress before or during delivery (one sure sign: sitting hunched with her nose in a corner of the cage), get help from a veterinarian or an experienced breeder immediately. If the sow is in hard labor for more than twenty minutes without a birth taking place, you also have a problem delivery. Rush her to the vet or cavy breeder. With the help of special instruments (like forceps), a trained person can often save both infants and mother. A cesarean section, surgery to remove fetuses from the uterus, is rarely successful, probably because the sow is in such a weakened condition by the time the attempt is made. Veterinary attention can also repair damage to the uterus that may occur during delivery. (For example, part of the birth canal may follow the fetus outside the body. When this, called a prolapse, or other damage happens, antibiotics will also be given to prevent infection.)

One other problem, a fetus in an improper position for delivery, is relatively common. A veterinarian can gently manipulate the baby so that he is correctly aligned for passage down the birth canal.

You can help out if the babies arrive so quickly that the mother neglects one or more of them. If the baby

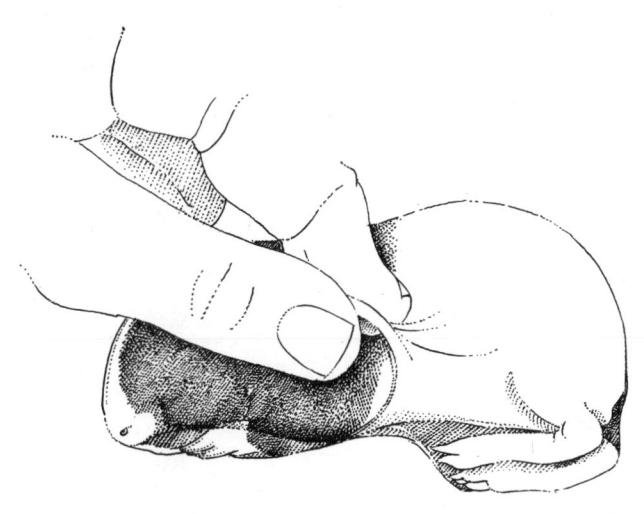

If the mother won't take care of her young, it's up to you to quickly peel the sac from the baby's face.

hasn't been cleaned by the sow, he may suffocate with the thick birth sac membrane over his face and oxygen no longer coming to him from the umbilical cord. To prevent this from happening, reach slowly into the cage and peel the membrane from the baby's face. This membrane may be a little "yucky," but you will be saving a life, so don't be squeamish. After the deed is done, place this newborn close to the sow, where she can see him. As long as all the babies are warm and breathing strongly, they'll be in no danger while waiting for the mother to start cleaning them.

Occasionally, an infant is not breathing after the sac is removed. This may be due to inhalation of some of the amniotic fluid. Lay this baby across the palm of your hand. Support the chin with your index or first finger and place your thumb on the crown of his head. Lay your other hand gently over the top of the baby to hold him firmly in place. Then shake the cavy upside-down in a quick HARD motion, almost a jerk. (Be sure to

Support a newborn's neck, back, and head before you shake or rub him down.

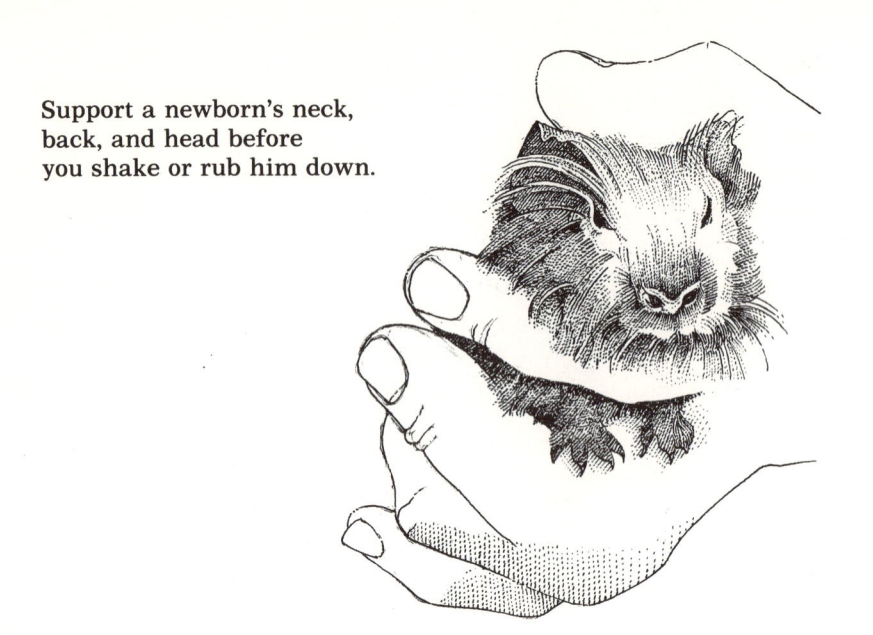

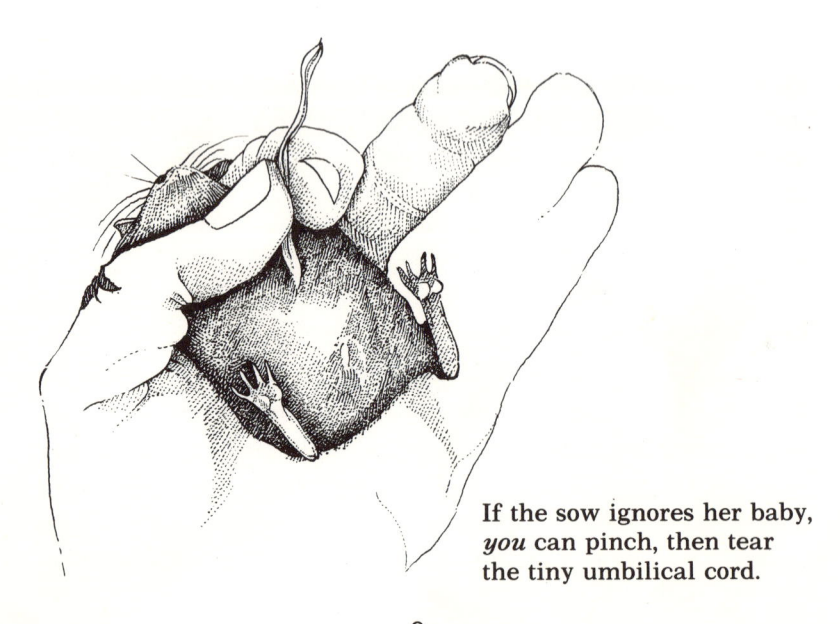

If the sow ignores her baby, *you* can pinch, then tear the tiny umbilical cord.

support the head and neck. Without this support, the motion can snap the little neck.) Sometimes fluid in the lungs can be cleared in this way and the youngster saved. If he begins gasping, rub the body vigorously with a rough towel. This will stimulate both circulation and respiration, as well as dry the baby.

Should the sow not be interested in cleaning her babies after delivery, the burden will fall on your shoulders. After you remove the membrane from the baby's face, clean the whole body with a warm dry towel. Then, *tear* the umbilical cord—cutting with a sharp instrument causes more bleeding than tearing. Do this by pinching the cord close to the cavy's body with two fingers of one hand (or with a hemostat—a clamp—which you can buy at a medical supply store), all the time supporting the baby's body in the palm of the same hand. With your other hand, use two fingers to grasp the cord just a little farther away from the cavy's body, twisting and pulling the cord until it separates.

If you are the one trying to save the baby, don't give up—even after several minutes of rubbing and shaking. You may be greatly rewarded for your efforts. Remember, however, that nature and the sow are a capable team. Don't get involved unless there's a real need. Have patience and watch!

TAKING CARE OF BABY

Newborn cavies are precocious. They are born fully furred, with wide-open eyes, alert to their surroundings. Within a very short time, they will explore the cage, nibbling at pellets and hay and sampling the water. They need to be fed, of course, but in most cases the sow provides sufficient nourishment by nursing her

A sow will stare into space contentedly while babies take turns at her two teats.

babies herself. Even a large litter of six will usually be nursed without troubles, each baby taking a turn at the mother's two teats. However, if you want to provide extra nutrition for a large litter and to relieve the sow of some pressure and strain, supplement the sow's milk with commercially prepared milk substitutes, such as Esbilac, Unilact, Calf Manna, or any one of several others, available from supermarkets, veterinarians, feed stores, and pet shops. Or you can use almost any breads, white or whole wheat, for example; cereals (cooked, such as Cream of Wheat or farina, or dry, such as corn flakes); and liquid or powdered milk. After about three weeks of nursing, the babies have, by themselves, gradually increased their intake of their mother's diet and decreased their nursing time to a point where they can be totally weaned. You may want to ease this independence from the mother by feeding the weanlings a milksop for the first day or two.

In the unfortunate case when the sow does not survive, you'll be left with orphan cavies to raise. When this happens, I usually try to find another sow who is nursing her own litter. This happy mother will almost always be willing to take any number of cavy babies, regardless of age or breed, and treat them as her own. In fact, if you have more than one sow, you should try to breed them to deliver at the same time, since they will, at times, assist each other during delivery, clean and wash each others' babies, and nurse each others' youngsters with complete disregard for family relation. This "nursery" syndrome can be used to relieve nursing pressure, especially when you can mix breeds of sows that tend to have small litters (Peruvians, for example) with breeds that tend to have larger litters (Americans).

However, if you have motherless cavies and no sow to substitute as a nursing mother, *you* can raise the babies by hand-feeding them a liquid formula. It's pos-

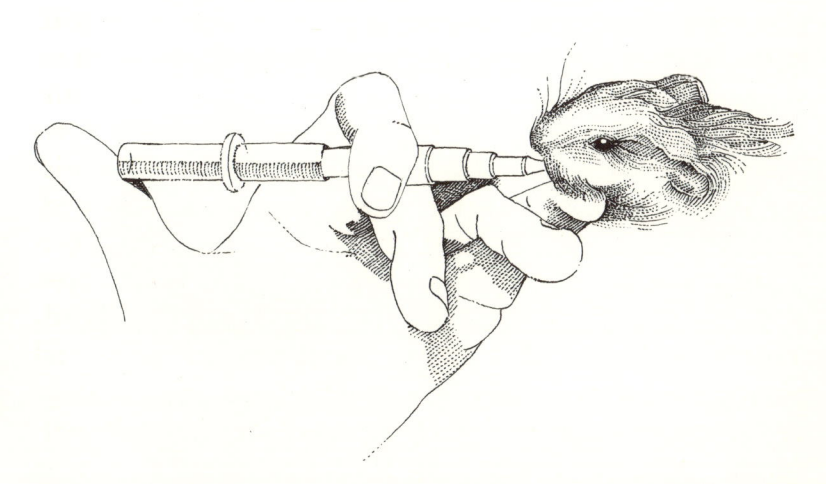

Keep the baby in an upright position when feeding with a syringe.

sible to do this with an eyedropper, but there's some danger of drowning a baby cavy by forcing too much formula into the mouth at once. It's safer, therefore, to use a feeder that holds a smaller amount and regulates the flow of liquid more exactly. A tuberculin syringe (*without* a needle), easily obtained from your veterinarian, works especially well.

What formula should you feed your orphan cavy? Almost every breeder seems to favor a different concoction. I prefer lukewarm Unilact mixed with a few drops of corn syrup. Some breeders use the following mixture: one tablespoon of evaporated milk, two tablespoons of warm water, one tablespoon of corn syrup, and a dash of Tang or pediatric vitamin C. Another breeder endorses a mixture of tepid milk, V-8 (vegetable) juice, and a drop of baby vitamins in a proportion of two-thirds milk and one-third juice when first given, with the amount of juice increased daily until the cavy is receiving two-thirds juice and one-third milk.

How much to feed? A whole tuberculin syringe holds a total of one cc. of fluid. A teaspoon holds five cc. of fluid, so you can see that you need to "think small." Measurements are marked on the syringe. Feed each cavy .25 cc to .5 cc. of formula to start. If he willingly finishes it off, give him a little more. This should be given every two to three hours during the day and through the evening (you don't have to get up from bed throughout the night). Put the drops on the front of the tongue. Never jam the syringe deep into the baby's mouth: he might inhale the liquid. As the youngster gets stronger, he will increase his intake by actually sucking from the syringe at his own rate, so you won't have to touch the little plunger. He will even come to demand his meals, squeaking at the top of his lungs to gain your attention. For the first week, grind or mash the pellets or grains that would be the mother's normal diet. Leave fresh water and bits of bread or cereals at all times. Hand-raising infant cavies is probably the most rewarding of feats since few other animals are as independent at birth. Because of this independence, the mortality rate of orphan cavies is relatively low and the success rate of raising them by hand very high.

FAMILY PLANNING FOR CAVIES

If a boar and a sow are allowed to share a cage all the time, the sow will probably be breeding constantly—a bad idea. Constant breeding shortens a sow's life span. She gets downright worn out, without a chance to regain the strength and vitality that are drained away in pregnancy, delivery, and nursing. Yet a sow that is not bred often enough will get overly fat from just sitting in her cage, overeating. Obese sows have more delivery problems (such as pregnancy toxemia) than those of trim weight (one and a half to two pounds). Before breeding your cavies, check the sow. If she is overly pudgy, reduce her intake of hay or treats and increase the living space she has. Perhaps you could put food at one end of her cage and water at the other so that she is forced to move about more.

And you'll want to regulate your sow's breeding by removing the boar from time to time. It is important, above all, to remove the boar before a sow gives birth. If left in the cage, the boar will not harm the babies. In fact, he will snuggle the babies just as a mom would do. But, if the boar is on the premises, the sow is likely to become pregnant again within hours after delivery when she experiences a postpartum heat. In order to prevent this, I usually remove the boar about sixty days after the time he and the sow first began sharing the cage—if she is heavily pregnant. And I keep the two separated until twenty-four hours after delivery. The sow should be over her postpartum heat by this time and will not become pregnant when the pair is reunited. A few weeks later, when the babies are weaned, she will be ready again to breed, her estrous cycle beginning about four days after weaning. Remove the boar once more to give the sow a well-deserved rest.

No sow should have more than four litters a year. Two or three litters a year are usually plenty, but it really depends on the weight and condition of each individual. Since a healthy sow can continue to breed for three or four years or longer, there'll be more than enough litters to please any breeder.

THE GOLDEN RULES OF BREEDING

1. Let nature take its course in pregnancy and delivery.
2. Be aware and ready to help out if something goes wrong. (It rarely does.)
3. Don't hesitate to get expert assistance for serious pregnancy problems.
4. Decrease the chance of *any* problems by providing a healthy diet, a clean home, and a calm atmosphere for the mother-to-be.
5. And—share the joy and excitement!

6
PREDICTING THE OFFSPRING: HOW TO GET WHAT

Why were you born with blue eyes, or brown, or green? Why is a puppy born with floppy ears or ears that point straight up? Why is a guinea pig born with a smooth black coat or a rosetted beige one?

The answer is heredity. Whether guinea pig or human, babies are born with traits, or physical characteristics, that are passed along to them from their parents. How these traits are carried from generation to generation is what genetics is all about. It can be a vast and complicated subject. But just a *little* knowledge of genetics can add another dimension to cavy breeding. Once you understand a few basic principles, it's possible for you to predict what sort of babies a guinea pig mother and father are *likely* to produce. However, until you are familiar with these rules, it would be wise for you to consult with a local breeder or your science teacher, who may have some specific knowledge in this area.

A LITTLE SCIENCE GOES A LONG, LONG WAY

Parents pass on family traits to their offspring through sub-microscopic structures called genes. Genes are present in each cell of an animal's body. There are separate genes, a pair, for each trait (in cavies these characteristics include size, shape, color, and coat texture, to mention just a few). When a cavy baby is conceived, he or she receives one gene from each parent for every trait.

It's simple, of course, to predict what will happen if the gene received from the mother and the gene received from the father are the same: for instance, if the gene for eye color from the father is pink and the eye color gene from the mother is also pink, the baby guinea pig is sure to have pink eyes. But what happens when the gene from the mother and the gene from the father are different? Will one gene triumph over the other, or will there be some sort of compromise between the two? The answer depends on how strong each particular gene is. Some genes—the gene for dark eyes in cavies, for example—are especially strong and are called dominant genes. Other genes—the gene for pink eyes is one—are weaker, and they're called recessive genes. In each particular case, if you know which genes are dominant and which are recessive, you can predict what the outcome will probably be. Let's take one situation as an example. If one parent contributes the gene for dark eye color while the other parent contributes the gene for pink eye color, you'll expect the baby cavy to be dark-eyed, because the dominant dark-eyed gene will win out over the recessive light-eyed gene.

Sometimes, however, when two genes for the same trait have different strengths, one gene does not totally dominate the other, producing what is called a hybrid. You can see this in the case of coat length by looking at the offspring from a Peruvian/Abyssinian crossing. The babies will be neither long-haired nor short-coated, but mid-length fluffies. This incomplete dominance may also occur when two recessive genes meet: one gene may or may not be more recessive than the other. So, if you breed a cream and a white cavy, for example (the genes for cream and white both being recessive), chances are that half of the offspring will be cream and half will be white.

Does this all sound relatively easy? It is, so far. But there's one other important thing you need to know: you can't always tell just by looking at the parents what gene a father or mother cavy is going to pass on to the baby. Remember that every father or mother was once a baby, a baby that received a gene for every trait from each of *its* parents. Therefore, if a cavy is black, it may be a pure black cavy—carrying two genes for blackness (one from each of its parents)—or it might also be a hybrid black—a cavy carrying both a dominant gene for blackness and a recessive gene for some other color. It is a matter of chance that determines which gene will be passed on to each offspring. That's why you can't be sure, just because the cavy is black, that it's going to pass on the gene for blackness to its baby. And sometimes it takes more than one pair of genes to determine a trait, such as color.

So, as you can see, unless you know all about the baby's grandparents and great-grandparents (called its pedigree), there may be some surprises when your sow and your boar have babies. But even if you can't be sure of the offspring just by looking at the parents-to-be, genetics—and the experience of cavy breeders—can help you to make fairly accurate predictions.

PREDICTING THE KIND OF COAT YOUR CAVY WILL HAVE

The coat of a guinea pig can come in a variety of textures and lengths—smooth, wiry, coarse, swirled, with special rosettes and/or ridges (see chapter 1).

Breeders' experiences have shown us which coat genes are dominant (rosette and crested) and which coat genes are recessive (long hair; short, smooth hair; and even more recessive, wiry, coarse hair), as well as what kinds of coats can be expected when various cavy breeds are mated. Here are the most common breeding combinations:

1. *If you breed an American cavy (smooth, short coat) with another American,* the offspring will almost always be a smooth-coated American. Why? Because if an American cavy were carrying the gene for a rosetted coat, a dominant gene, the swirls would show, and the cavy parent wouldn't look like an American at all. However, an American might be carrying a recessive gene for a short, smooth coat and a recessive gene for a coarse coat (the Teddy) or a longer coat (the Silkie). When two apparently pure Americans like this breed, they may occasionally produce a Teddy or a Silkie.

2. *If you breed a rosetted cavy (Abyssinian with medium-length hair and ten specifically placed rosettes, or Peruvian with an extra-long coat and only a few rosettes) with another swirl-coated cavy of the same breed,* the offspring should be swirl-coated, just like the parents. But smooth-coated animals are also possible. Since the gene for rosettes is dominant over the recessive one for a smooth coat, a Peruvian or Abyssinian parent may carry one dominant and one recessive coat gene. These parents can conceivably produce a smooth-coated baby (an American or Silkie). In order to get these results, of course, each parent has to have had an ancestor with the smooth coat in order to be able to pass on this recessive gene.

3. *If you breed an American cavy with a White Crested cavy,* the offspring may be either White

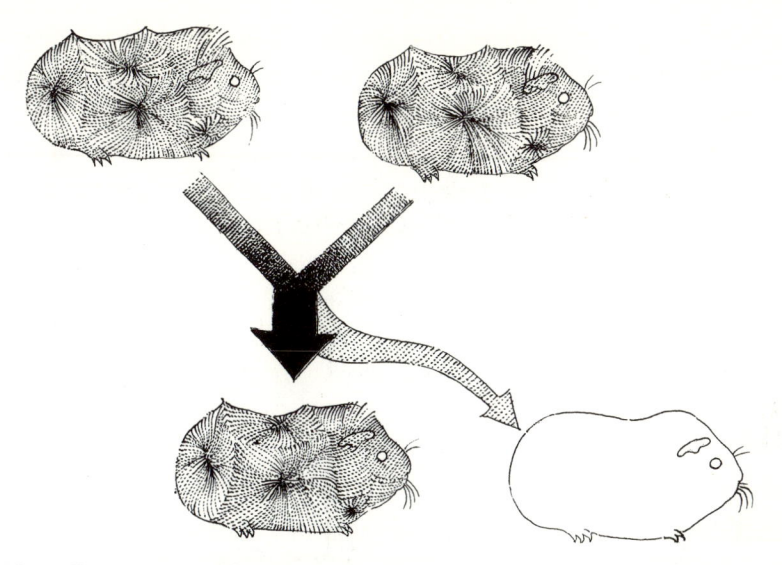

The offspring of Abby parents are usually Abbys, although short-haired Americans or Silkies are possible.

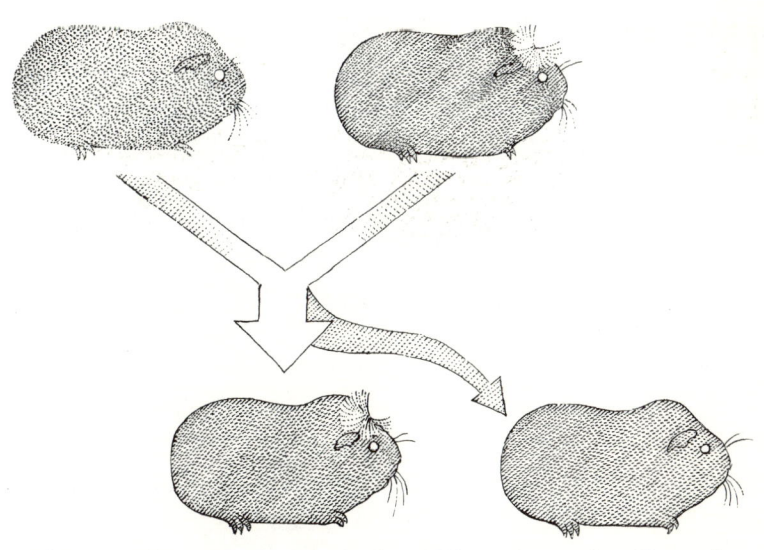

Breeding an American cavy with a White Crested will produce either American or White Crested babies.

Crested or American, depending upon whether the White Crested parent is a pure Crested (carrying two dominant Crested genes) or a hybrid one (carrying one dominant Crested gene and one recessive American gene). Teddies can also appear from this breeding if there are Teddy ancestors on each side and each parent has passed on the recessive gene for the kinky coat.

What about the next generation? Since the rosette gene is dominant over the smooth-coated gene, American youngsters resulting from an American and a White Crested mating will produce only Americans, never White Cresteds, since they have received only the genes for a smooth coat from each parent. White Crested cavies, however, from American/White Crested parents can produce both White Crested and American offspring in future generations because they are carrying the recessive smooth-coat trait.

4. *If you breed an American cavy with a coarse-coated Teddy,* the resulting youngsters will all be hybrid Americans, since the gene for the coarse, kinky Teddy is overpowered by the gene for smooth coat. Not one of the offspring of such a mating will have a coarse, wiry coat unless there were, somewhere back in the American pedigree, Teddies (or at least one) on each side. Any of these hybrids could produce pure Teddies when bred to a Teddy. If you breed two hybrid Americans, you will also find some pure Teddies in the resulting litter.

5. *If you breed an American cavy with a rosetted Abyssinian,* neither coat gene will be totally dominant. Youngsters will be mixed breeds, or mongrels, fitting in none of the recognized breed categories. The coats may look very much like smooth American coats, but they will be marred by either a ridge of hair on the back

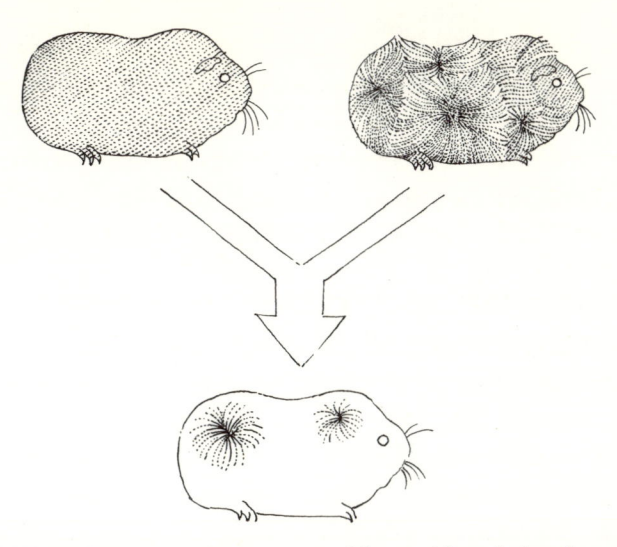

The mating of an American cavy with an Abyssinian is not ideal, since it results in mongrels, sometimes called hybrids or mixed breeds.

(very much like a human cowlick that, no matter what you do, cannot be brushed flat) or an occasional haphazardly placed rosette. The coat will be too coarse to be an American's, but far too soft for an Abyssinian's. This is not the best of matings unless you are trying to establish your own breed because it is almost impossible to predetermine the results.

6. *If you breed an Abyssinian with a long-haired Peruvian,* the results will again be mongrels, none of which will resemble either parent—one youngster may have longer hair, one many rosettes, another a coarse, shorter coat, and so on. Not only will the Abby's neat and orderly rosette patern, which serious fanciers strive to produce, be disturbed and destroyed, but the long, graceful Peruvian coat will also disappear and be replaced by a mixture of long and short hairs that re-

semble rooster tail feathers. Experienced breeders call this type of cavy, in which neither coat gene totally dominates the other, a Fluffy or a Rooster.

7. *For the most predictable results, breed American to American, Abyssinian to Abyssinian, Peruvian to Peruvian, and so on.* If you do this type of breeding, you will be carrying on the work of many earlier breeders and fanciers who first developed these unique breeds. Perhaps you will be the one to evolve the perfect guinea pig, the one that most closely resembles the ideal described in the *Standards of Perfection.*

Or you may enjoy creating the unusual brand of guinea pig. If so, crossbreeding is for you. Who knows, you may be able to create and standardize a new breed. Serious fanciers have worked hard over the years developing the recognized breeds. Originally there was only one; today there are six. And in the future?

PREDICTING WHAT COLOR YOUR CAVY WILL BE

Most of us know from casual observation that cavies can be found in a great array of colors. The combinations seem to be limitless: black, chocolate, red, cream, beige, white—so many! Yet, genetically speaking, there are only two colors, black and yellow, with black the dominant one. How is this possible? How can our eyes see what scientists say isn't there? Well, the answer is relatively easy. The colors *are* there, but they are all derived from either of the two basic colors. There are two substances called pigments that determine, by their presence or absence, coat color. When a cavy has the maximum amount of these pigments—eumelanin (black and brown) and phaeomelanin (yellow and red) —in his coat and skin, he is black. If only phaeomelanin is expressed, the animal will be red or cream. If neither is expressed, the animal will be white. The various combinations of these pigments are determined by genes, which influence other aspects of color as well, such as depth of color and patterns. Some common examples of this include the agouti, with two different colors on each hair; the roan, with its even intermingling of white and black or white and red hairs; and the tortoiseshell and white, which has clear-cut patches of red, black, and white.

Below is a partial list of possible colors. The varieties

Selfs (one body color)	*Solids or Marked* (two or more colors)	*Ticked*
beige	broken color	agouti (in many shades)
black	brindle (red and black)	
blue	Dalmatian (white with clear pigmented spots)	
chocolate	dapple (white with spots marked with white hairs)	
cream	Dutch (black or red body, white feet, collar, blaze)	
golden	Himalayan (white body, black smut on nose, black feet, socks, and ears) roan (red or black with white)	
lilac	tortoiseshell (black and red checkerboard)	
orange (bright red) with pink eyes	tortoiseshell with white (black and red checkerboard with added white patches)	
red		
white		

can conceivably be found in all the breeds, although some are not acceptable for showing. Most of the colors can be found in combinations with others (chocolate and cream, for instance), or with white (red and white or black, white, and red to name just two).

There are too many possible cavy colors and too many delicate differences in shadings, markings, and spottings to list all breeding combinations. However, there are some general guidelines to help you and some warnings to keep in mind.

1. *Dark colors contain more dominant genes than lighter colors.* When dark- and light-colored cavies are mated, more dark-colored babies than light ones can be expected. Although there are exceptions, the general rule is that you can get light colors from dark parents, but not dark colors from light-colored parents.

2. *Some colors are only partially dominant.* Broken color animals (red/white, cream/white, agouti/red/white, chocolate/cream, to mention a few) bred to solid animals will usually produce babies that are mainly one color or another with a touch of the second color. Perhaps there will be a white foot or nose on a red body or a tiny patch of cream on a chocolate one. If nicely spotted babies are your goal, find and use two parents with even, clear patching.

3. *Breed selfs with solids and other selfs.* Solid-colored cavies, such as the roan or brindle, will produce offspring with a better mix of colors when they are bred with selfs. For example, solid black bred with a blue roan yields deep blacks and blue roans. Red bred with a red (strawberry) roan yields rich reds and strawberry roans. Brindles and roans are also good breeding pairs because, in both cases, the colors tend to blend evenly. *Never breed a roan to a roan!* (See guideline 7 below.)

4. *Breed broken colors with tortoiseshell and white.* This will produce offspring with clear, sharp, attractive patching, an improvement in the variety. To make sure this happens, avoid breeding cavies that have brindled (mixed-colored) patches or those with no sharp dividing line between these patches.

5. *Do not breed tortoiseshell and white or broken colors with roans or brindles.* The offspring often have huge patches of white and less than 50 percent roan, a disqualification from the show table. Or you may get brindle and white animals, another undesirable combination at shows.

6. *Do not breed selfs or solids with broken colors or tortoiseshell and white.* The offspring often have a solid-colored body with a white snip on the nose or a few white toes. They will rarely have the beautiful, even distribution of color you are striving for.

7. *Never breed roans with other roans!* The babies resulting from a roan-to-roan breeding may suffer defective teeth and blindness. These unfortunate youngsters can be recognized by their white coats, small, pink, rotated eyes (eyes that are turned partially up into the head, rather than looking straight outward as guinea pig eyes do), and missing or misshapen teeth. They rarely survive more than a few weeks—certainly only a short time after weaning. These babies are products of what is commonly termed the "lethal" gene: two genes for the roan coloration.

TRICKS OF THE TRADE

You don't have to get serious about breeding. It's fine if you want to breed just for the fun of having some babies around. But if you *do* intend to take breeding seriously—either for the fascination and the challenge, or for the purpose of showing, or both—you'll want to keep in mind some basic approaches, some neat techniques, and some special hints.

1. *Pick your breeding couple with care. Be a creative matchmaker.* Before pairing your cavies, observe them carefully. If your sow has a pointed face, find her a mate with a nicely rounded head. If your boar has small eyes, find him a sow with large bold ones. Ideally, the babies from these pairs will get the better qualities from their parents. If you breed two cavies with the same faults, the babies stand a good chance of inheriting those faults. When one mate has a good point, such as nice bold eyes, to balance off the poorer trait, there is a strong possibility of improving the quality of your animals. Remember: pointed noses seem to be dominant over rounded ones, although not totally; short hair is at least partially dominant over long hair; and dark colors are dominant over light ones.

When picking a mate for your cavy, try to find one that has as good or better traits than yours. Here one has beautiful bold eyes but folded ears, while the other has wonderfully drooping ears but tiny eyes.

2. *Become familiar with the* Standards of Perfection *for your breed.* If you're interested in showing your cavies, try to breed so that an offspring's traits will be closer than its parents' traits to the ideals of the particular breed. Avoid breeding cavies that have undesirable traits that may reappear in offspring and disqualify them from shows—an extra toe on the hind foot or an extra teat, for example.

3. *Use* line breeding *and* inbreeding *to achieve a desired trait.* If you are working to perfect a particular breed or variety, you can best produce cavies of improved quality by using a single family—or genetic line—of cavies, beginning with a boar or sow that has the desired trait. Suppose, for example, that you want to breed Teddies. You got a Teddy boar for a gift and have no idea where to get another Teddy, since they are quite rare. Start out with your boar and breed him to more than one American sow, since Americans are very closely related to Teddies genetically. Next, when these babies are old enough, breed the offspring of the one family with the offspring of the other. Then, for the third generation, breed only the pure Teddies to each other. If at this point you do not have enough Teddies to breed several pairs, you can breed a hybrid Teddy with a full Teddy.

If you do not have enough cavies to start line breeding (say you have only a boar and a sow) or even if you do, a quicker way to obtain pure Teddies is to breed close family members (inbreeding), such as father with daughter, mother with son, or brother with sister. Since undesirable traits, long hidden because of their recessiveness, may be produced with inbreeding, strict culling should be practiced, using only the best animals for future matings.

Sample Breeding Record Card

Name: Flower   Breed: Abyssinian   Variety: brindle

#	bred to	color	date bred	litter born	description and number of offspring
1	Blacktop	black	3/21/81	5/26/81	(3) roan boar, roan sows
2	Coke	brindle	7/30/81	10/9/81	(4) brindles: 2 boars, 2 sows
3	Sam	blue roan	2/8/82	5/1/82	(2) tri roan boar, brindle boar
4	Blacktop	black	9/20/82	12/5/82	(2) black sow, roan sow

FRONT

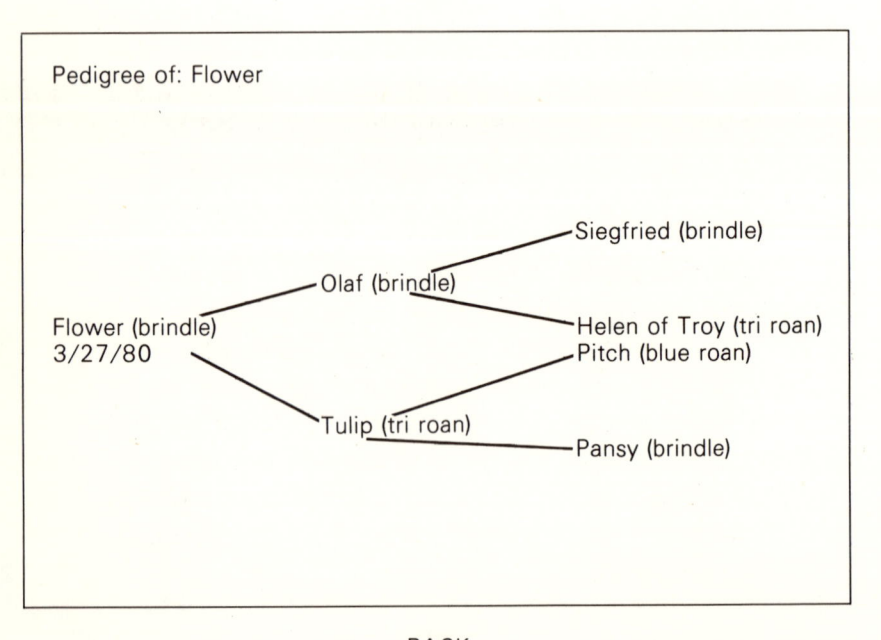

Pedigree of: Flower

Flower (brindle) 3/27/80
- Olaf (brindle)
  - Siegfried (brindle)
  - Helen of Troy (tri roan)
- Tulip (tri roan)
  - Pitch (blue roan)
  - Pansy (brindle)

BACK

One caution, however: though both line breeding and inbreeding will certainly result in pure and perfect traits, they may also result in loss of size, vigor, and fertility over a long period of time. If such losses occur, you'll want to add a non-family member to the breeding program—this is no problem as long as the newcomer has the same traits that you're breeding for.

4. *Use breeding record cards and genetic squares.* Record full breeding descriptions of each litter. This will help you see patterns and be able to better predict the basic outward appearance of offspring. By tracking your cavies' ancestries, you will be aware of what recessive as well as what dominant genes potential parents may be carrying.

The breeding record card can be as simple as a three-by five-inch index card. On the front you can write the

Sample Show Record Card

Name: Flower   Breed: Abyssinian   Variety: brindle   Born: 3/27/80

date	show	judge	# in class	place	special awards
6/30/81	New York State	Long	4	1st	best brindle
7/14/81	Rochester Rabbit Breeders Association	Dumbleton	6	2nd	
11/28/81	Chemung Rabbit Breeders Association	Steele	3	1st	best brindle
9/11/82	North Country Rabbit Breeders Association	Eisel	4	1st	best brindle, best opposite sex Abyssinian

pedigree and a list of breedings and litters, or use both sides for this. On the reverse side or on a separate card you can list the show record, if there is one. Show records are important in order to know which are your best animals for breeding. An impressive show record will also help you sell your cavies at a better price. It is great if you can tell a prospective buyer of the wins made by his new pet's parents. Other breeders will also be interested in the show record when they need new animals for their breeding programs.

If you know the background of a cavy pair, a genetic square can help you to determine the possible results of their mating. Once you are familiar with which genes are dominant and which recessive, a genetic square can be used to predict many of the traits cavy breeders are interested in: type of coat, color, texture, shape, and so on.

Here is a simplified genetic square. Keep in mind that some traits, such as coat color, are complicated. Many pairs of genes may determine the total trait, each pair affecting only a part, such as depth of color, ticking, or shading.

1. Draw a square and divide it into four equal boxes inside.

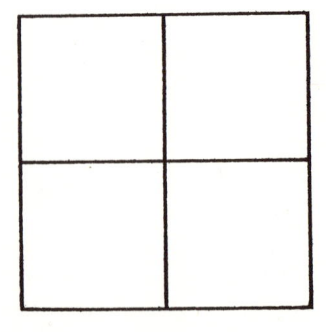

2. Say you would like to predict the kind of coat the offspring of two American cavies, both half Teddies, are likely to have. Mark the two coat genes of each parent along the side of the square.

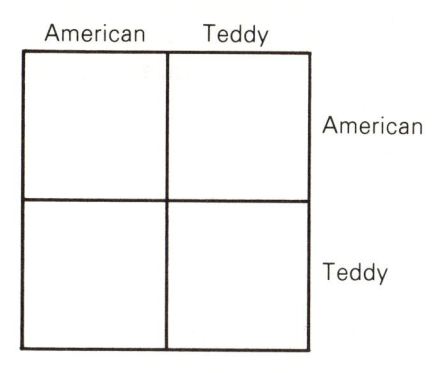

	American	Teddy
American		
Teddy		

3. Match one gene from a vertical column with another from a horizontal column, and list both in each empty box. From this you can see that you have a one-in-four chance of having pure-bred American or Teddy offspring and a two-in-four chance of producing Americans that carry the recessive Teddy gene.

	American	Teddy
American	American/American	Teddy/American
Teddy	American/Teddy	Teddy/Teddy

You can also use this square for predicting general color traits. If, for example, you breed two black guinea pigs, each having had a Himalayan parent, a genetic square will show you that one baby in four will be pure black, one will be pure Himalayan, and two will be hybrid blacks, carrying the recessive gene for Himalayan. Of course, many traits are determined by more than one gene, so the results predicted by this simple genetic square will not always come to pass.

	B	h	
B	BB	Bh	
h	Bh	hh	

B = black

h = Himalayan

THE DOUBLE FUN OF GENETICS—SCIENCE AND SUSPENSE

If you become interested in breeding scientifically, you'll want to learn as many of the methods of planning and prediction as well as production as you can. But don't be too surprised if a cavy baby should turn out to be the complete opposite of what you expected. Mutations, or "sports"—a variety never seen before, a first-time-ever combination—occasionally show up in a litter. That's the suspense part of genetics. You may feel, as some cavy owners do, that genetics is something you don't want to be bothered with, or you may enjoy exploring the subject in every fascinating detail. If you find you're hooked and want to learn more about breeding, the sources listed at the back of this book are good references for further information.

7
SHOW TIME!

Most people don't know—and sometimes people won't believe—that there are cavy shows just as there are horse and dog shows. In some areas, New York and California to name two, there are as many as twelve shows a year. Exhibitors often travel for hours, sometimes in caravans, to shows a great distance away. There are also shows in Canada, open to American exhibitors, and there's a national convention, as well as mini-conventions sponsored by the American Cavy Breeders Association, by state and county fairs, and by 4-H groups.

What happens at a cavy show? Well, there are, of course, judgings of cavies in various categories—breed, variety, class (age and sex)—and awards are given to the cavies that come closest to meeting the ideal standards. But shows are also social occasions, opportunities for cavy owners and breeders to meet and to talk about their problems and their successes. Ideas are exchanged, and so are guinea pigs—all in the interest of better cavies and cavy breeding. Newcomers are always made to feel welcome, no matter what age they are. Travelers from far-off towns are often provided with accommodations; camaraderie develops along with friendly competition. Since there aren't as many cavy owners, breeders, or show people as there are for animals like dogs, cats, and horses, individual cavy lovers really count.

GETTING READY FOR THE SHOW

Should you plan on entering your cavies in a show? There's only one way to make that decision: check out the competition. Become familiar with descriptions and photographs of cavies considered to be outstanding, then compare the front-runners with your own pets. Study the description of the ideal cavy of each breed in the first chapter of this book and the *Standards of Perfection*. Consult breeders and other owners in your area. Compare their cavies with yours. Do you think yours are good enough to compete?

If you do, find out where and when the nearest cavy show is to be held—and plan for it. Contact your local rabbit club (cavy shows, especially in New York State, are often held in conjunction with rabbit shows), write to the ACBA, or get in touch with your local Agricultural Extension service. The phone number for this last group can be found in the white pages of your telephone directory, along with other county governmental services. The county 4-H office should be listed in the same place. For most shows, there'll be an entry form to be sent in some time before the competition (for ACBA shows, there's always a catalog for the show, with an entry form included). Fill in the form, pay any entry fee (these vary and can be as low as fifty cents per animal or as high as several dollars), and you're ready to go.

But that doesn't mean you just sit at home and wait until show time. There's a lot you can do to prepare for the show, especially since you want your cavies to be in superb condition when they're presented to the judge. First of all, in addition to making sure, as always, that your cavies are getting nutritious, vitamin-rich food, you'll want to keep your guinea pigs particularly clean and free of lice and mites. Judges will disqualify cavies that are heavily infested with lice or mites, sometimes even if there's only a slight indication of infestation. Furthermore, such parasites often lead to rough, bare spots in a cavy's coat and will be heavily penalized at shows. So keep your cavies well-dusted with cat flea powder or some other small-animal lice and flea powder. (*Do not* use any powder or spray intended for dogs since these are far too toxic for our more delicate little critters.)

Achieve both cleanliness and soft coats by bathing your guinea pigs regularly, with extra-special baths. Using warm water and either tearless baby shampoo or kitty flea shampoo, wash and rinse all traces of dirt away. Do this just a few days before the show for all cavies except the Abyssinians and Teddies. These two breeds need time without a bath, perhaps as long as two weeks before the show, so that their coarse, wiry coats can develop the right texture and not be too soft. So bathe your Abbys and Teddies at least two weeks beforehand, and then keep them dry, clean, and dusted; you'll have to powder them to keep them free of parasites.

Grooming is the other major area of preparation for cavy shows. Some breeds need virtually no special grooming at all. The short-coated Americans do require some attention: their coats must be kept even and smooth by periodically removing the hairs that grow unusually long (guard hairs). To do this, place the cavy so that he faces you; then grasp a small amount of his hair from his back or rump between your first finger and your thumb. With the other hand, gently pull out any extra-long hairs, pulling just a few at a time and always pulling away from you, toward the cavy's rear

Keep your short-coated cavy's coat even by plucking the guard hairs.

end. If done properly, this procedure shouldn't bother the animal at all.

It is the long-haired Peruvian and Silkie breeds that really require extra grooming care. To keep their ever-growing hair out of the way of toenails and teeth, you must keep their coats tied up in wrappers. These must be removed once a day or every other day so that the coat can be combed out; otherwise they may irritate the cavy, causing him to chew his wrappers and his coat right off.

HOW TO WRAP THE PERUVIAN AND SILKIE COATS

1. Set the cavy on a table in front of you and gently comb all the hairs with a wide-toothed comb until the coat is completely smooth. If there are any mats, carefully separate the hairs with your fingers. Never just pull with the comb. Use a soft baby brush next, being sure to smooth the bottom layer of hair as well as the top. Part the hair down the middle of the animal's back from just behind the head to the start of the rump.

2. You will be using one wrapper for the frontal (none for the Silkie), two on each of the side sweeps, and one or two on the rear sweeps, depending on the length and thickness of the hairs.

3. Cut paper toweling widthwise into two pieces so that you have two wrappers from each towel.

4. Fold each half sheet of toweling in half, long sides together.

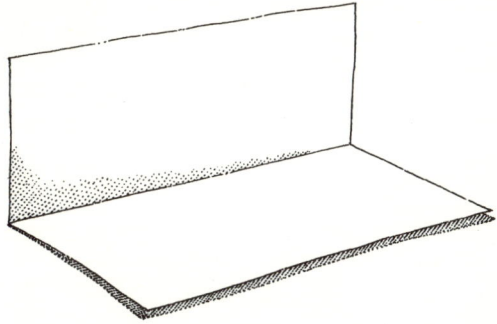

5. Take the frontal in your hand, smooth it out, and slide or place the ends between the folded paper, slightly to one side.

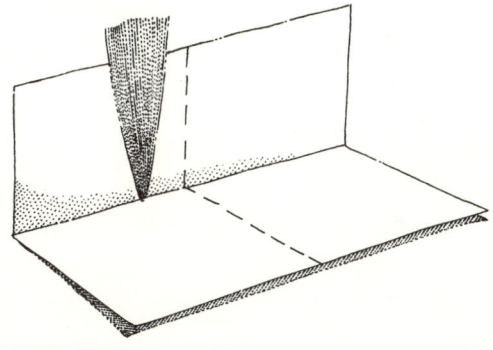

6. With one hand hold the paper and the frontal securely but gently. You do not want your cavy to jump around because you are pulling a few hairs. With the other hand, fold the paper in half again, short sides

together. Then fold in half once more, bringing the toweling beneath the frontal so it is well padded on both sides.

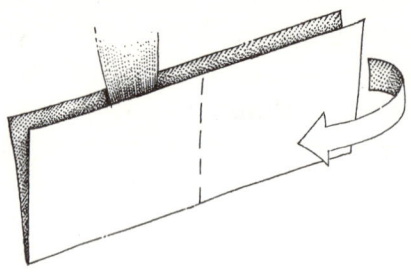

7. Fold this packet of hair and toweling lengthwise toward the body and secure the whole thing with a rubber band.

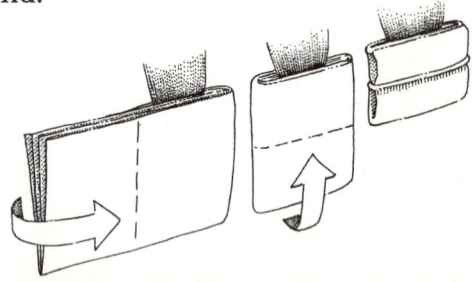

8. As the hair grows longer and longer, you will need to increase the size of the paper.

9. Repeat this procedure for each of the side and rear sweeps.

10. Before you put your cavy back in its cage for the day, always check to see if any little hairs are being pulled. (If you have ever had braids or ponytails you know how much one pulled hair hurts.) A cavy will not tolerate any discomfort from his wrappers and will chew off the distressful paper, hair and all.

The comb-out of a Peruvian or a Silkie serves a double purpose. First of all, of course, it keeps the cavy's coat smooth and beautiful. Use both a soft-bristled brush (a human baby brush will do fine) and a hard-bristled brush (a wide-toothed wire dog brush is best, not a slicker brush or a human hair brush) to brush the coat. Comb out layer by layer—don't just brush the surface—and make sure that you get down to skin level. Do everything gently, without the sort of vigorous strokes that remove gobs of hair. Then, using a wide-toothed dog comb, comb the coat outward from a center point in the middle of the back. When viewed from above, the Peruvian should have a totally even, symmetrical appearance, while the Silkie's coat should take on a teardrop shape. After the comb-out, use endpapers to

The Peruvian (left) and Silkie show coats can be as long as or longer than eighteen inches.

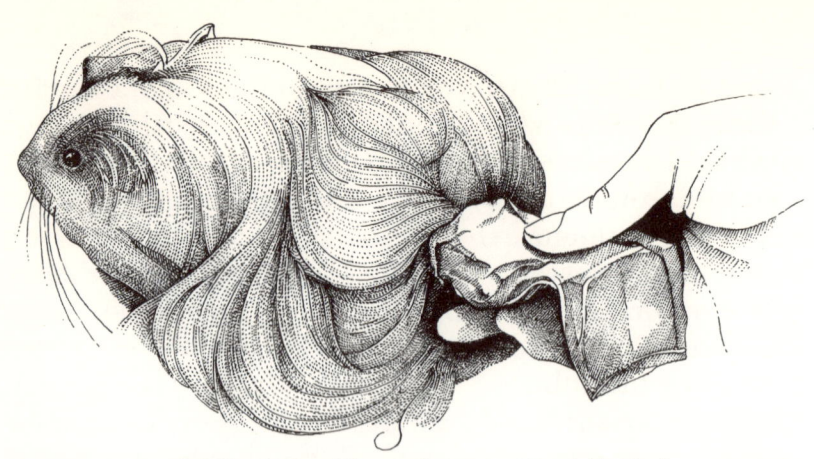

Peruvians and Silkies should stand very still while their coats are groomed and wrapped.

rewrap the coat—either three wrappers (one on each side sweep, one on the rear sweep) or five to six wrappers spaced evenly around the sweeps and frontal (if there is a frontal). The number of endpapers is a matter of preference and usually depends on the length and thickness of the coat.

The comb-out of a Peruvian or a Silkie has a second function as well: it gets the long-haired cavy used to standing still, which is what is expected of these breeds at cavy shows. And since guinea pigs find the comb-out a highly pleasant experience, once they are accustomed to it, you should have no trouble training your cavy to stand still during daily or every-other-day grooming. Whenever he moves too much during the comb-out, simply lay your hand over his back and the top of his head. Then press downward gently—he'll get the idea in no time.

Finally, there's one more way to get prepared for a show. While some shows are cooped—ones that provide display cages called coops—many others are carrying-case shows. At a carrying-case show, your cavy will spend all his time in the box he arrives in, except for those moments when he takes his place on the judging table. Therefore, your carrying cases had better be comfortable. In summer, prepare wire cages with shavings on the bottom—they'll be cool and airy. During cold, damp weather, be ready with warmer boxes made of wood or cardboard. In either case, always remember to bring along your own pellets, hay, and water, so that you can minimize the stress that transport and new, unfamiliar surroundings will have on any cavy, especially older ones.

SHOW TIME!

Whether you send in an entry form in advance or fill it out when you arrive at the show, there will always be six main categories in which to enter your cavies—one for each of the six recognized breeds. Within each of the breed categories, there are separate divisions for different varieties of the breed. Within each of those divisions (Red, Abyssinian, for example), there are six classes of sex and age: Senior Boar, Senior Sow (over six months old and more than thirty-two ounces); Intermediate Boar, Intermediate Sow (four to six months old and twenty-two to thirty-two ounces); Junior Boar, Junior Sow (under four months old and less than twenty-two ounces). Showing a cavy less than six weeks old is not recommended; these youngsters are not able to compete against mature juniors because of their tiny size and baby shape and soft coat. Entry forms will have spaces for you to list your cavy's breed, variety, and class.

Once your cavy is registered, he'll be assigned a number, which is then written down on adhesive tape and placed on his right ear. Permanent ear tagging—at-

Cavy Entry Blank

(please type or print)

Coop No.*	Ear No.	Breed	Variety	Sex	Check One Sr. Int. Jr.	Entry Fee	Specials
	N-42	ABBY	ROAN	BOAR ✓		1.00	

Total Amount Enclosed __1.00__

*superintendent will fill in coop number

It is hereby understood and agreed that these animals are entered at owner's own risk and that the show management will not be responsible for the entries, though all due care will be used to protect them.

I make the above entries subject to the rules of your show.

Enclosed is __1.00__ for my entries.

Name of Club __U.S. CAVY CLUB__
Date __7/20/82__
Exhibitor __HARRIETT RUBINS__
Address __105 MADISON AVENUE__
City __NEW YORK__ State __N.Y.__ Zip __10016__

Entry Number

taching a numbered metal tag to the cavy's left ear like a staple—has been a requirement at ACBA shows since January 1980. For this, metal mouse tags are painlessly clipped into the animal's ear and become the cavy's lifetime identification number. These numbers can be used to register your animals with the ACBA, and these registered guinea pigs can compete for the title of Grand Champion, a much-sought-after honor. The numbers on these ear tags are so tiny, however, it is sometimes difficult for the judges to read them. This is the reason the second number and adhesive tape are used, in hopes of making the show move along more quickly. Both the permanent ear tags and the taped numbers can be put on at the show before show time by an experienced fancier, who will be happy to "show you the ropes." Now comes the judging.

Judges are hired by the host club. Depending upon the number of entrants, there may be one or more than one judge. To become a judge you must study the rules and regulations governing shows and the standards for each breed. After an apprenticeship with several qualified judges, you are eligible to take the test for a judging license. Judges are likable people usually willing to talk to new fanciers and old about almost anything, AFTER the competition is ended. However, you must be quiet at the judging table, never asking a neighbor, "Is that one yours?" A judge wants to be impartial. Any animal whose owner is identified may be excused from the table and the rest of the show.

Cavies are examined at a high table, one that enables the judge to inspect the animals thoroughly without endless bending over. (A judge with a backache can be pretty grumpy!) The table, which usually has a number of separate holding compartments, is most often covered with a rug to prevent the cavies from slipping and sliding. All the cavies competing in a certain class—sometimes even all the cavies in a variety, if there are only a few—are brought to the judge simultaneously, carried to the table by "carriers," not by the cavy owners. (In this way, there's no chance of the judge's being influenced by personal feelings about one owner or another.)

The judge will examine your competing cavy carefully. If he finds temporary conditions, such as abscesses or pregnancy, lice or respiratory disease, he will eliminate your cavy from this particular competition—but the cavy will be eligible for future competitions once the condition has returned to normal. If, however, the judge finds undesirable permanent conditions—say, extra toes or teats—he will disqualify your cavy from the competition. You are expected to keep such an animal out of any other cavy shows, since any judge who finds the disqualification will also remove him. In such cases, you will be wasting your time and money.

If your cavy is neither eliminated nor disqualified, then he or she will be further examined and judged, feature by feature, trait by trait. The judge will be following the accepted guidelines for how an ideal cavy of each breed should look, stand, and act. (These guidelines are described, breed by breed, with drawings and photographs, in the American Rabbit Breeders Association's booklet, *Rabbits and Cavies—Standards of Perfection*. See page 132.) He or she will award points for each feature—quality of color, coat length, coat texture, condition, size, shape, and so on—taking into consideration both positive and negative aspects of your cavy's traits.

If your boar or sow comes closest to the Standards of Perfection for the particular class, he or she will win for that class, and then go on to compete against all the other class winners in that variety. If your cavy should be chosen Best of Variety, the next competition will be for Best of Breed, with all the different Best of Variety winners competing against each other. Finally, all the Best of Breed winners compete for the Best in Show award—usually a trophy plus a very small cash award.

For example, you enter your cavy Patch in his class —American, Senior, Broken Color (chocolate/cream/

Patch's Pathway

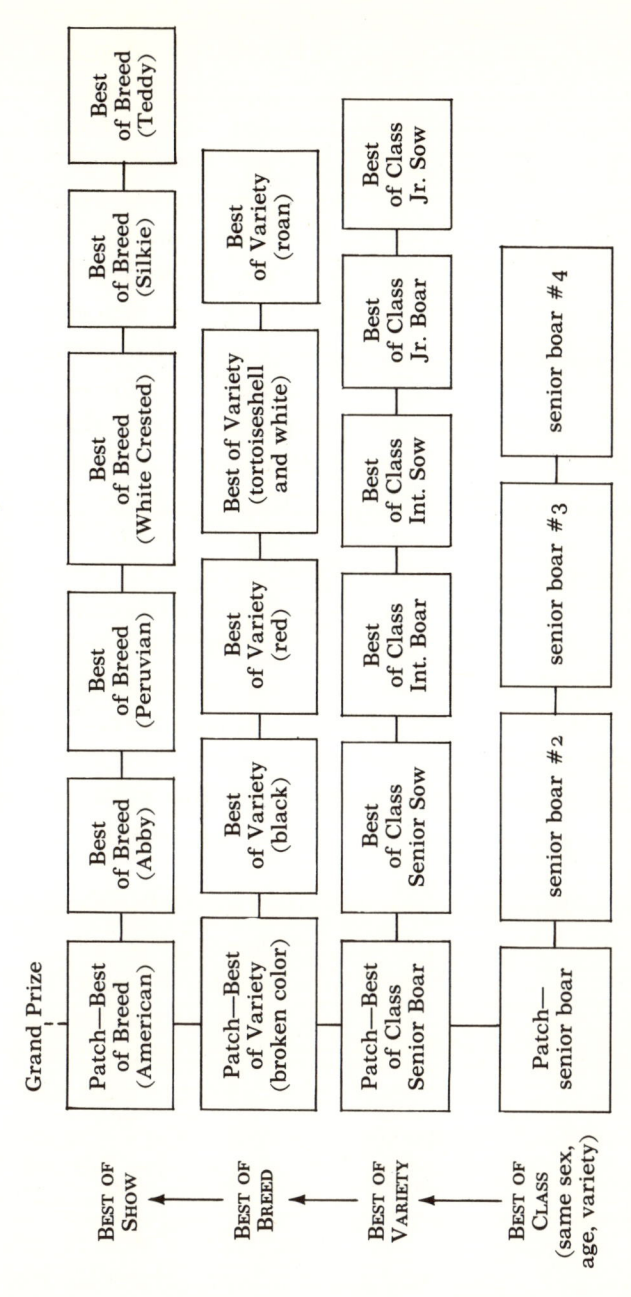

Grand Prize

Patch—Best of Breed (American)	Best of Breed (Abby)	Best of Breed (Peruvian)	Best of Breed (White Crested)	Best of Breed (Silkie)	Best of Breed (Teddy)

Patch—Best of Variety (broken color)	Best of Variety (black)	Best of Variety (red)	Best of Variety (tortoiseshell and white)	Best of Variety (roan)

Patch—Best of Class Senior Boar	Best of Class Senior Sow	Best of Class Int. Boar	Best of Class Int. Sow	Best of Class Jr. Boar	Best of Class Jr. Sow

Patch—senior boar	senior boar #2	senior boar #3	senior boar #4

← BEST OF SHOW
← BEST OF BREED
← BEST OF VARIETY
← BEST OF CLASS (same sex, age, variety)

Patch = American, broken color, senior boar

Sample Judging Form

Coop No. _____   Ear No. __N-42_____
Entry No. _____   Weight_____

Breed __ABBY_____
Class & Sex __ROAN, SR. BOAR_____
No. in Class __7_____   Award __1ST_____

SCORE CHART

	EXCELLENT	GOOD	FAIR
Type	✓		
Ears		✓	
Head		✓	
Color	✓		
Condition	✓		
Coat		✓	
Bone			
Shoulder			✓
Saddle			
Hind Qtrs.			

Judge's Remarks __LARGE, WELL BALANCED BOAR — GOOD COARSE COAT AND PLACEMENT OF ROSETTES, NICE LARGE BOLD EYE_____

Place __U.S.A._____
Date __7/20/82_____

white), Boar. He is brought to the table with three other senior, broken color boars. The judge loves him and gives him a first place. Later on in the judging, Patch will compete again, this time against the Best Senior

Sow, Intermediate Boar and Sow, and Junior Boar and Sow—all Broken Color Americans. Once again he is victorious, being awarded the title of Best of Variety. His next competition will put the winner of every color against your Patch: black, red, tortoiseshell and white, roan, and so on. Of course, your pet is so terrific he wins Best of Breed. Now, in the finale, Patch will compete against the Best Abyssinian, Best Peruvian, Best White Crested, Best Teddy, and Best Silkie for the Best in Show award and the Grand Prize. We won't pick out a winner at this time, because this whole example is only an if, a maybe, and a wish. But it would be nice, wouldn't it?

Throughout the competitions, the judge not only awards points, but also explains his opinions of the competing cavies. This running commentary ("Good eyes, fair ears, excellent crown") is a terrific way to learn what judges look for and what you should look for as you try to improve the quality of your cavies. You can also gain show experience by participating in the judging process—as a carrier or as one of the secretaries who records the judges' comments on official cards. You'll learn from this that within the standard guidelines different judges emphasize different features: one may demand pinpoint rosettes in Abyssinians, while another may stress perfect ridges and collar. You'll discover, too, that color may be highly important to the competing strength of one breed (Americans, for example) while hardly important at all to the winning potential of another breed (for Peruvians, the length, texture, and density of the coats are the top priorities).

Don't be disappointed if your cavy isn't a winner at every show or if he isn't perfect; there are very few perfect animals in this world. Even if you don't win a prize—at cavy shows everyone usually wins *something*

—it's a great chance to meet people, to get experience, to sell your extra guinea pigs, or to buy new cavies of high quality.

Find out about cavy shows in your area and then show off!

8
WANT MORE INFORMATION?

IMPORTANT ADDRESSES

>American Cavy Breeders Association (ACBA)
>c/o Robert Leishman, Secretary
>6560 Upham
>Arvada, Colorado 80003

Write the ACBA for information on cavy shows, for information on how to join the organization (members receive a useful magazine), and for the rules and regulations for cavy shows. This organization can put you in touch with the cavy breeders nearest your hometown.

>American Rabbit Breeders Association (ARBA)
>1925 South Main Street, P.O. Box 426
>Bloomington, Illinois 61701

Write the ARBA for information on cavy shows and for their publication, *Rabbits and Cavies—Standards of Perfection*. They will be happy to send you a complete price list for their publications, membership, and other items they have for sale, such as pedigree forms. This organization can also put you in touch with breeders in your area.

>Ontario Cavy Club
>c/o Bruce Eisel
>R.R. #7
>St. Thomas, Ontario N5P 3T2
>Canada

This club puts out an excellent magazine and maintains a large inventory of cavy items, such as books, pamphlets, articles, decals, and shirts with cavies on them.

There are many other good cavy clubs throughout the United States and the Commonwealth countries, including the New York State Cavy Fanciers, New England Cavy Club, Rocky Mountain Cavy Club, and the Golden State Cavy Breeders Association (California). The ACBA can give you these addresses if you write to it.

BIBLIOGRAPHY

American Rabbit Breeders Association. *Rabbits and Cavies —Standards of Perfection.* Bloomington, Illinois: American Rabbit Breeders Association, 1981–1984. This volume is updated every four to five years.

Hutchinson, Patricia. *Guinea Pigs: Their Care and Breeding.* Leicester, England: K. and R. Books Ltd., 1978.

Lane-Petter, W. *Animals for Research: Principles of Breeding and Management.* New York: Academic Press, 1963.

Midgley, Ruth, ed. *Pets: Every Owner's Encyclopedia.* London and New York: Paddington Press, 1978.

Musselman, Virginia W. *Learning About Nature Through Pets.* Harrisburg, Pennsylvania: Stackpole Books, 1971.

Potter, George, and W. Lane-Petter, eds. *Breeding Laboratory Animals: Notes for Breeders of Common Laboratory Animals.* Jersey City, New Jersey: TFH Publications, Inc., 1962.

Silverstein, Alvin and Virginia. *Guinea Pigs: All About Them.* New York: Lothrop, Lee and Shepard, 1972.

Sole, Alan. *Cavies.* London: Cassell and Collier, Macmillan Publishers Ltd., 1975. (Can be purchased from the Ontario Cavy Club.)

Turner, Isabel. *Exhibition and Pet Cavies.* Hampshire, England: Spur Publications Co., 1977.

For further study of genetics, read *Color Genetics of the Cavy,* a booklet available from the author, Catherine Whiteway. Her address is Langley Cottage, Lower Langley, Wevelscombe, Somerset TA4240, England. The price may change so consult the author about cost.

Glossary

abscess • an infection usually caused by bacteria that takes the form of a lump or nodule, most often found in the neck or chin region of the cavy. It is usually filled with a thick whitish-yellow or greenish pus.

agouti • the coloring of the original cavies found in South America. There are two different colors on each hair shaft, except for the belly hair, which does not have different colored ends.

alfalfa cubes • strands of hay compressed into one-inch or larger blocks. Made specifically for small animals to gnaw on, they're much neater than loose hay.

amniotic fluid • the liquid surrounding the fetus in the uterus that helps cushion it from the outside world.

antibiotic • a type of drug developed to combat particular bacterial infections.

anus • the opening to the rectum through which feces pass.

bacteria • one-celled microscopic organisms, some of which are necessary in the cavy's system to help its digestive process, others of which cause disease, such as pneumonia.

birth sac • a thick membrane that completely surrounds the fetus in the uterus.

boar • a male cavy.

breed • a type of animal that produces offspring just like itself. The six breeds of guinea pigs recognized by the American Rabbit and Cavy Breeders Associations are the American, Abyssinian, Peruvian, White Crested, Teddy, and Silkie. Used as a verb, breed means to produce offspring.

brindle • a cavy whose coat consists of an even intermingling of red and black hairs, giving an appearance of a single color.

carrying-case show • a cavy competition in which the animals remain in their carrying-case cages, except for grooming and judging purposes.

cataract • a disease of the eye in which the lens becomes opaque, causing partial or total blindness.

Cavia porcellus • the scientific name for guinea pig. The Latin word *Cavia* is thought to come from the South American Indian word "cabiai," used to describe various short-tailed and tailless rodents; *porcellus* is Latin for "little pig."

cavy • fanciers' and breeders' term for guinea pig.

cesarean section • the surgical procedure used by veterinarians to remove fetuses. Usually done when the sow cannot deliver her babies by herself.

class • for show judging, the category based upon cavy age and sex.

cloudiness • a condition of the cornea whereby the normally clear covering over the pupil of the eye turns gray and opaque.

coccidiosis • a highly contagious disease caused by the protozoa coccidia. The main symptom is diarrhea.

collar • in the Abyssinian cavy, a ridge of erect hair that circles the neck from shoulder to shoulder.

conception • the joining of egg and sperm in fertilization.

congenital • referring to a condition existing from birth.

conjunctivitis • an inflammation of the mucous membrane lining the eyelid and eyeball. The white of the eye appears pink and the eyelid area looks inflamed.

constipation • the inability to defecate or pass feces.

cooped show • a cavy competition in which exhibition cages are provided by the sponsoring group.

cornea • the transparent covering over the iris and pupil of the eye.

crest • a rosette found on the forehead of the White Crested cavy.

crossbreeding • the mating of two different breeds, such as an Abyssinian and an American cavy.

crown • the area just behind the top of the cavy head.

culling • eliminating undesirable parents from a breeding program.

dehydration • a loss of fluids from the tissues of the body. In cavies, this often occurs after or during a severe bout of diarrhea.

diarrhea • excessively loose bowel movements.

disqualification • in cavy exhibition, barring an animal from competition because of a condition, such as missing toes or an extra teat. There are two ways for an animal to be removed from a show: elimination is temporary; disqualification is permanent.

dominant gene • a gene that may dominate another in a pair.

egg • a female's reproductive cell that, when fertilized by the sperm, develops into a fetus.

elimination • in cavy exhibition, temporarily excusing an animal from competition because of a condition, such as abscesses, pregnancy, or parasite infestation. Once the condition is no longer present, the cavy can be exhibited at another time.

estrous cycle • in the female, the period of time it takes for the eggs to develop, mature, and be released for fertilization and for the sequence to begin again. In cavies, this process takes about seventeen days.

feces • excrement or waste released through the anus.

fertilization • the process whereby egg and sperm join, beginning the formation of offspring.

fetus • the developing, unborn offspring.

forceps • a grasping surgical instrument that resembles tweezers but does not have sharp ends. With problem pregnancies, forceps may be used to help deliver cavy babies.

fracture • a broken bone.

frontal • the section of long hair on the head of the Peruvian cavy that often covers the eyes and ears.

full term • in pregnancy, the amount of time it takes for the fetus to develop fully before being born. In cavies, this takes about sixty-three days.

fungus • a plant that has no leaves, flowers, or green color. Since it cannot produce its own food, it must get it from other sources. A fungus, such as ringworm, can be harmful because it feeds on living plants and animals. Other *fungi* (plural), such as mushrooms and some molds, are harmless, and may even be beneficial, because they feed on decaying matter.

genes • sub-microscopic structures that carry family traits from one generation to another. There are two for each trait, one from each parent, passed on to each offspring.

genetics • the science that describes how traits are carried from generation to generation.

gestation • the time from conception to birth.

guard hairs • the long loose hairs that extend beyond the rest of the cavy coat on the short-coated breeds, such as the American.

hybrid • offspring that has two different genes for the same trait.

impaction • a condition brought about by a large ball of feces blocking the anus, making defecating difficult or preventing it altogether.

inbreeding • the mating of close family members, such as brother to sister and parent to child.

incomplete dominance • in breeding, one trait that does not totally overpower another. For example, an Abyssinian bred to a Peruvian cavy will produce offspring with fluffy, medium-length coats, longer than the normal Abby coat but much shorter than the usual Peruvian length.

intermediate • any cavy four to six months of age and weighing between twenty-two and thirty-two ounces.

junior • any cavy under four months of age and weighing less than twenty-two ounces.

labor • the delivery process, from the time the uterus begins to contract until the baby is expelled from the body.

lice • tiny wingless parasites that can infest cavy hair and skin.

ligaments • tough connective tissues that hold bones together or keep organs in place.

line breeding • breeding family members together for several generations in order to produce certain characteristics.

litter • the total number of babies born in a given pregnancy.

mammary glands • the female organs that produce milk.

mane • upright hair found all along the Abyssinian cavy's neck, beginning between the ears and ending at the collar.

marked • spotted or patched coloration as in a broken color, Dalmatian, or Dutch cavy.

milksops • a mixture of bread or dry cereal soaked in room-temperature milk.

mite • a minute parasitic bug.

mixed breed • an animal having more than one breed in its background, such as the offspring of an American/Peruvian pairing.

mongrel • another term for mixed breed.

mutation • offspring unlike its parents that is the result of a change in the genes.

needle nose • the term used by fanciers to describe an undesirable, pointed face.

ophthalmic solution • medicated eye wash or drops.

oral • having to do with the mouth.

ovary • the female organ that produces eggs. Each sow has two ovaries.

parasite • an organism, such as lice or mites, that lives off another animal, called the host.

pedigree • ancestral record.

pellets • commercially prepared guinea pig diet formula in large granule form.

pigment • any substance that transmits color.

placenta • the organ (kidney bean-shaped, maroon colored) that supplies the fetus with nourishment and removes its wastes. It is located within the uterus, connected to the fetus by the umbilical cord. It is delivered with the baby.

postmortem • an examination to determine the cause of death.

postpartum heat • the time immediately following delivery

when the sow releases eggs for fertilization and so can become pregnant again.

prolapse • the slipping of an internal organ, such as the uterus or rectum, out of place. This may happen to a sow during delivery.

protozoa • a one-celled animal, such as coccidia.

pure • having two identical genes for the same trait.

pus • thick, whitish-yellow, sometimes greenish matter that is made up of bacteria, white blood cells, and serum and that is produced as a result of an infection.

rear sweeps • the long coat hairs that cover the rump of the groomed Peruvian and Silkie.

recessive gene • a weaker gene whose trait will not show up in offspring unless it is paired with another recessive gene for the same trait.

ridge • a line of upright hair formed by adjoining rosettes that is found on the Abyssinian coat.

roan • a cavy whose coat consists of an equal intermingling of either red and white or black and white hairs, giving the appearance of one overall color.

rodent • a group of mammals that includes the cavy, rat, hamster, woodchuck, and chinchilla. Rodents are characterized by continuously growing front teeth that are used for gnawing.

rosette • pattern formed by hairs radiating full circle around a center point—found on Abyssinian, Peruvian, and White Crested coats.

rump • the rear end of the cavy, beginning at the bend of the hips.

saddle • the middle of a guinea pig's back.

scurvy • the disease caused by a lack of vitamin C whose symptoms are loss of weight and muscle tone.

self • an animal that has one overall body color.

senior • any cavy over six months of age and weighing more than two pounds.

side sweeps • the extra-long coat hairs that grow down the sides of the groomed Peruvian and Silkie.

smut • the black coloring found on the Himalayan nose.
solid • a cavy variety that includes brindles and roans. Solids have coats made up of a mixture of colors that give the impression of a single color.
sow • a female cavy.
sperm • the male reproductive cell.
spore • a reproductive cell of microscopic organisms, such as coccidia.
sulfamethazine • a "broad spectrum" drug used to combat many bacterial infections.
teat • the nipple at the end of the mammary gland through which infant cavies and other mammals are nursed.
toxemia • a poisoning condition. In pregnancy toxemia, poisons from the uterus are sent through the bloodstream.
toxic • poisonous.
umbilical cord • a cordlike structure that connects a fetus to the mother's placenta and through which food and wastes are passed.
uterus • the female organ in which the fetus develops and grows.
variety • animal coloring.
virus • a sub-microscopic organism that can cause diseases such as pneumonia.
wean • to remove babies from a mother's company so that nursing is no longer possible.
weanling • a young cavy, just separated from a nursing sow, usually three to six weeks of age.
wrappers • special papers used to tie up and protect the long-coated Peruvian and Silkie.

INDEX

Page numbers in **bold** refer to illustrations

abscesses, 59–60, **59**, 124
Abyssinian ("Abby") cavies, 22–23, **22**, 28–29, 115
   breeding combinations and, 96, 97, 98–100
agouti (variety), 21, 31, 101
Agricultural Extension service, 114
ailments; *see also* specific conditions
   general symptoms of, 55–56
   isolation and, 56
   medications for, 57–58
   preventive medicine and, 53–55
allergies, 41, 65
American cavies, 21–22, **21**, 28–29, 115–116
   breeding combinations and, 96–100, 97, 109, **109**
   grooming and, 115
American Cavy Breeders Association (ACBA), 20, 26, 30, 31, 113, 114, 122, 124, 131, 132
American Rabbit Breeders Association (ARBA), 20, 131
amniotic fluid, 79, 83
antibiotics, 57, 58–59, 62, 63, 82
   side effects of, 57, 58–59
appetite, lack of, 56, 60
aquariums, 37, 39–40
   sunlight and, 40

babies:
   birth of, 81–82
   birth weight, 81
   breathing of, 83–85, **84**
   care of, 85–89
   cleaning of, 81, 85
   cloudiness of eyes, 64
   delivery problems and, 82–85, **83**, **84**
   diet of, 86
   formulas for, 88
   general appearance of, 85
   hand-feeding of, 87–89, **87**
   nursing of, 85–86, **86**, 87
   orphan, 87–89
bacteria, 61–62
bacterial infections, 57, 59, 60–61, 63
bathing, 115
beddings, for cage floors, 40–41, **48**
   allergic reactions to, 41, 65
birth, 81–85
   boars and, 80–81, 89–90
   breeding and, 81–85
   cesarean section, 82
   labor and, 81
   problems in, 76, 82–85
birth sac, 81, 83, **83**
boars, 32–33, **33**
   age for breeding, 76
   birth and, 80–81, 89–90
   weight for breeding, 76
bones, broken, 60
breeding, 75–90; *see also* babies, birth, pregnancy
   ages for, 76
   cage size for, 76–77

combinations, 96–100
conception in, 76–77
constant, 89–90
crossbreeding, 100
culling and, 105
factors to consider before, 75–76
fertilization in, 75, 77
genetics and, 93–110
guidelines for 90, 104–105
inbreeding, 105, 107
line breeding, 105, 107
record cards and genetic squares for, **106**, 107–110, **107**
weights for, 76, 89
breeds, 20–30
    table of, 28–29
brindles, 31, 101
    breeding combinations and, 102, 103
broken color, 31, 101
    breeding combinations and, 102, 103

cages, 37–42, **39**, 53
    bedding for, 40–41
    cleaning of, 37, 61, 62, 70
    cost of, 37–38, 40
    fish-crate, 38
    flooring for, 37, 39, 40–41
    glass, 37, 39–40
    for shows, 120–121
    wood vs. metal, 37–39
carrying, *see* handling
carrying cases, 42, **42**, 56, 120–121
cataracts, congenital, 64
Cavia porcellus, 18
cavies, *see* guinea pigs
cavy clubs, 131–132
cesarean section, 82
checkups, 53
chewing on coat, 65–66
cloudiness in eyes, 64
coats:
    breeding combinations and, 94, 95–100
    shedding of, 17
    wrapping of, 116–120, **117, 118**

coccidiosis, 60–61
colds, 61–62
coloring, *see* varieties
conception, 76, 77
conjunctivitis, 63–64
constipation, 63
coops, 120
Coronation cavies, 30
cortisone, 58
cotton balls, 58
"creeping dandruff," 67
crossbreeding, 100
culling, 105

Dalmatian cavies, 31, 101
death of cavy, 70–71
dehydration, 47, 56, 62
delivery of babies, 81–85
diarrhea, 45, 48, 57, 58, 60, 62–63
    causes of, 45, 48, 57, 58–59, 62
    diet for, 62
    greens and, 47–48
    medications for, 58, 62–63
    molds and, 65
diet, 45–49
    of babies, 86, 88–89
    balanced, 49
    cavy vs. rabbit pellets in, 46
    for diarrhea, 62
    for pregnant sow, 77
    vitamin C in, 45–47
    water in, 45
dispensers, for water, 45, **46**
drooling, 66, 69
Dutch cavies, 31, 101
dystocia, 82–85

ear infections, 63
ear tagging, 121–123
eggs, 77
estrous cycle, 77, 90
eye drops, 58, 64
eye problems, 63–64
eyewash, antibacterial, 58, 59, 64

flea and lice powder, 58, 67, 115
flooring, cage, 37, 40–41

141

Fluffy cavies, 100
food; *see also* diet
  alfalfa cubes, 48, 49
  fruits, 47
  grains, 45, 46, 47, 68, 77, 86
  grasses, 42, 46, 47, 48
  greens, 47–48, 66, 67, 69, 77
  hay, 45, 48, **48**, 49
  horse-sweet feed, 47
  liquid formula, 87–88
  milk, liquid or powdered, 86
  milksops, 49, 77, 86
  milk substitutes, 86
  pellets, 45, 46, 49
  "people" food, 49
  vegetables, 47
  water, 45
forceps, 82
4-H groups, 113, 114
fractures, 60
fungal infections, 64–65

genes, 93–110
  coat color and, 100–103
  coat length and texture and, 94, 95–100
  dominant, 94, 96
  hybrids and, 94, 95
  incomplete dominance and, 94–95
  "lethal," 103
  recessive, 94, 96
genetics, 93
  basic principles of, 93–95
genetic squares, 107, 108–110, **109**
gestation period, 77
glossary, 133–138
grooming, 23, 24, 25, 26, 115–120
  wrapping coats and, 116–117, **117**, **118**
guard hairs, 115–116, **116**
guinea pigs (cavies):
  adoption of, 17
  as all-purpose pets, 13–14
  breeds of, 20–30
  classification of, 19–20, **19**
  companionship for, 33, 55
  costs of, 17, 24
  death of, 70–71
  diet of, 45–49
  factors in choosing, 16–18, 34
  feeding costs of, 17
  general appearance of, 16, 20, 34
  history of, 18
  housebreaking and, 16–17
  official scientific name of, 18
  other pets and, 16
  personality of, 14, 18, 20
  sex of, 32–33
  sounds of, 14, 18, 20
  varieties of, 30–32

hair loss, 65–66, 67, 77
handling:
  of cavies, 16, 53, **54**
  of pregnant sows, 78, **78**
hand-raising, of orphan cavies, 87–89
hay, 45, 48, **48**, 49, 63, 65
head tilt, 63
heat exhaustion, 41, 66
heat reactions, 66
heat stroke, 41
heredity, 93; *see also* genes, genetics
Himalayan cavies, 31, **32**, 101
  breeding combinations and, 110, **110**
housing, of cavies, 37–42, **39**, **42**; *see also* cages, carrying cases, wooden cage
  heat and, 40, 41, 66
  indoor vs. outdoor, 41–42
  sunlight and, 40, 42, 66
  temperature for, 37, 41–42, 53
  ventilation and, 40, 41, 42, **42**, 53, 66
humane societies, 17
hybrids, 94, 95, 99

illnesses, *see* ailments
impaction, 66–67
inbreeding, 105–106

142

incomplete dominance, 94–95
infections, 48, 57, 59, 61, 62, 63–64
isolation, in illnesses, 56

"leakers," 39–40
lice, 58, **64**, 67, 115, 124
lifting, *see* handling
line breeding, 105–106
listlessness, 56, 60

marked (variety), 31, 101; *see also* broken color, Dalmatian, Dutch, tortoiseshell, tortoiseshell and white
mammary glands, 60
medications, basic, 57–58, **57**
  storage of, 57
milk, 49, 86
mites, 58, **64**, 67, 115
mixed breeds, 98, **99**
molds, 65
mongrels, 76, 98, 99, **99**
moving, 55
mutations, 20, 110

"nose in the corner" syndrome, 56
"nursery" syndrome, 87

ointment, antibacterial, 58
Ontario Cavy Club, 131
ophthalmic solutions, 58, 64
ovaries, 77

pedigree, 95, 108
pellets:
  cavy, 17, 45, 46, 67
  purchase of, 49
  rabbit, 46, 49
  storage of, 49, 67
  substitutes for, 47
  vitamin C supplement in, 46, 49, 67
penicillin, 58
Peruvian cavies, 23–25, **24**, 28–29
  breeding combinations and, 96, 99–100

coat comb-out for, 23, 24, 25, 118–119, **119**
  wrapping coats of, 23, 116–117, **117**, 119–120
pet shops, 17, 37, 40, 48, 49
pigments, 100–101
placenta, 79, 81
postpartum heat, 89
pregnancy, 75, 77–81, 124
  changes in sow's body during, 77, 78–79
  conception in, 76–77
  diet for sows during, 77–78
  gestation period, 77
  problems in, 66, 69, 76, 79–80
  risks of, 75
pregnancy toxemia, 80, 89
prolapse, 82

rabbit clubs, 114
rabbit pellets, 46, 49
Ridgeback cavies, 30
ringworm, 64–65
roans, 31, 101
  breeding combinations and, 102, 103
Rooster cavies, 100
rubbing alcohol, 58

Satin cavies, 30
scurvy, 49, 67–68
selfs (variety), 30, 101
  breeding combinations and, 102
shows, 113–127
  categories and divisions in, 113, 121
  cooped vs. carrying case, 120–121
  disqualification from, 124
  ear tagging in, 121–123
  elimination from, 124
  entry forms and fees for, 114, 121, **122**
  judging in, 123–127, **126**
  preparing cavies for, 23, 114–121
Silkie cavies, 21, 26, **27**, 28–29
  breeding combinations and, 96, **97**

143

Silkie cavies *(cont'd)*
   coat comb-out for, 26, 118–119, 119
   wrapping coats of, 116–117, **117**, 119–120
solids (variety), 30–31, 101; *see also* brindles, roans
   breeding combinations and, 102
sows, 32
   age for pregnancy, 75, 76
   birth and, 81–82
   diet during pregnancy, 77
   estrous cycle, 77
   weight for pregnancy, 76, 89
sperm, 77
"sports," 110
Standards of Perfection, 25, 100, 105, 114, 124
starvation, teeth and, 69
steroids, 58
stress, 55, **59**, 78, 121
sulfa drugs, 57, 60, 61
sunlight, 40, 66
sunstroke, 66
syringes, 58, **87**, 88

Teddy cavies, 26, **27**, 28–29, 115
   breeding combinations and, 96, 98, 105, 109, **109**
teeth:
   broken, 68
   improper alignment of, 69
   overly long, 68
   starvation and, 69
   uneven, 68
tortoiseshell, 31, 101
tortoiseshell and white, 31, **32**, 101
   breeding combinations and, 103
traits, 93

traveling, 42, 56
tumors, 60

umbilical cord, 79, 81, 83, **84**, 85
uterus, 77, 79

vaccinations, 53
varieties, 20, 30–31, **32**, 101–103; *see also* agouti, marked, selfs, solids
   breeding combinations and, 94–95, 100–103
veterinarians, 56, 60, 61, 62, 63, 69, 70, 80, 82
viral infections, 61, 62, 63
vitamin C, 45–46, 47, 66, 77
   in cavy pellets, 46, 49, 67
   food sources of, 46
   pediatric liquid, 47, 68, **68**
   scurvy and, 49, 67–68
   water soluble, 66
vitamin D, 77
vitamin deficiencies, 45, 66, 67–68, 69
   in sow's pregnancy, 66, 77–78

"wasting disease," 69
water, 45, 49
   crocks, 45
   dispensers, 45, **46**
weakness, 66, 69
weanling, 33, 86
weight loss, 69
White Crested cavies, 25, **27**, 28–29
   breeding combinations and, 96–98, **97**
wooden cage, 37–39, **39**
   how to make, 38–39
wound ointments, 58, 69–70
wounds, 69–70
wrappers, 23, 24, 116–118, **117**–118, 119–120